# TRUTH IS ONE

*Truth is one: sages call it by various names.*

—Rig-Veda I, clxiv, 46

# TRUTH IS ONE

*The Story of the World's Great Living Religions*
*in Pictures and Text*

HENRY JAMES FORMAN AND ROLAND GAMMON

HARPER & BROTHERS   *Publishers*   NEW YORK

Art Director: SAYRE ROSS

Picture Research Assistant: HUGO BLOCK

The selection from *The Ten Principal Upanishads*, put into English
by Shree Purohit Swami and W. B. Yeats, Copyright, 1937, is
reprinted by permission of The Macmillan Company.

Library of Congress catalog card number: 54-8950

# CONTENTS

# FOREWORD

THE MAINSPRING OF THE strength in any race or people lies in its spirituality. The death of that people begins when its spirituality wanes and materialism becomes dominant. For religion is the greatest motive power on earth, far exceeding any other force in releasing the infinite energy in man that is like a coiled spring, waiting to be freed. To study the great religions, therefore, or at least to know something about them, would appear to be a paramount necessity.

The great dichotomy, the division between science and religion, has thinned out almost to the vanishing point—all in the space of half a century. Recent·scientists, like Sir James Jeans, find the universe "to look more like a great thought than a great machine." Similarly, Sir Arthur Eddington, physicist and astronomer, among the most eminent, declares that "the stuff of the world is mind-stuff." "I regard matter," he said, "as derivative from Consciousness." The old atheism is gone with the old materialism. The physicists especially are obliged to discard it. "I believe in God . . ." said Albert Einstein, "who reveals himself in the orderly harmony of the universe." The world is not a chaos but a cosmos. To Professor Robert A. Millikan, another great American physicist, "God is the *Unifying Principle* of the universe. No more sublime conception has been presented to the mind of man, than that which is presented by Evolution, when it represents Him as revealing Himself, through countless ages, in the age-long inbreathing of life into constituent matter, culminating in man with his Spiritual nature and all his God-like powers."

This spiritual nature, these God-like powers, which even great scientists attribute to us, we hazily know that we possess. But to most of us, this knowledge remains little more than hearsay all the days of our lives. Even a cursory examination of the great religions, however, convinces us that realization of the divinity that is within us and all about us is an experience which many have achieved, and one which is possible for every one of us. It is a mystery, yet a mystery open to anyone who will pause long enough to solve it. It is a secret, yet a secret that is cried from the housetops, if only we heed the call above the deafening worldly din. Others have solved it, others have heard it. Our race clings to the possibility of this realization, as witness the living religions it has clung to for hundreds and thousands of years.

Another truth of the utmost importance to us of today is that the great religions are not contradictory or antagonistic in themselves. Only man makes them so. But even man is dimly beginning to realize that there is no sense in this antagonism. More and more people point out, as though in wonder, that the Golden Rule is common to all great religions. Why should it not be, since the aim of all religions is the same? They are all phases of the one eternal religion that may at times suffer partial eclipse, but never dies. There is, in brief, beneath the superficial diversity an essential unity that is one of the most thrilling discoveries we make. An eternal harmony runs through all. How much we could enhance that harmony by dropping antagonisms and, instead, showing sympathy for all! Race, climate, geography, all these affect the details, but in essentials the great religions coincide. We may have different visions of the same truth, but the truth is one.

Again and again someone discovers that we are all one world. The multiplicity of phenomena, the endless variety of life, makes us forget this fact. It makes us forget that we are all one creation, that the brotherhood of man and the Fatherhood of God are so patently obvious, only some strange blindness prevents our seeing it. "Finite beings," said the late Professor Josiah Royce, one of America's leading philosophers, "are always such as they are in virtue of an *inattention* which at present blinds them to their actual relations to God and to one another."

Well, we are those "finite beings," and ours is the inattention and also the blindness. The religions of the world are the optical treatments attempting to remove the blindness. What person possessed of intelligence (almost, we were going to say, possessed of his senses) can fail to be interested in humanity's age-old techniques for removing our cataracts and curing our blindness? To give a succinct story of each of the great religions, to present them as vividly as possible through the use of striking pictures and a clear, uncomplicated text, is the object of the present book. The world is waking up, however slowly, to the fact of its own unity. Over and over we have heard that "no man liveth unto himself. . . . We are all members one of another." The time is not far off when this must be universally realized, lest we perish from the face of the earth.

Our debt to all the scriptures of the world and to how many authors, both living and dead, is so vast that we cannot even attempt to enumerate them. We can only express our gratitude. One of these, Dr. Bhagavan Das, of India, in his truly encyclopedic book on *The Essential Unity of All Religions* (Ananda Publishing House, Benares), quotes "The Anthem of the Universal," from the *World Fellowship*:

> One Cosmic Brotherhood,
> One Universal Good
> One Source, One Sway,
> One Law beholding Us,
> One Life enfolding Us,
>     In Love alway.
> Lust, Greed, Fear, Envy and Hate
> Long made us Desolate.
>     Their reign is done.
> Race, Color, Creed, and Caste,
> Fade with the Nightmare Past,
> Man wakes to learn at last,
>     All Life is One!

# 1. HINDUISM

## *Truth is one: Sages call it by various names*

THE HINDUS LAY CLAIM TO having the oldest religious philosophy in the world.

They are probably right. For long before the Christian era, before ever the Hebrews made their Exodus out of Egypt, perhaps even before Abraham came out of Ur of the Chaldees, the Vedas, the most ancient Indian scriptures, already existed.

These Vedas, especially the Rig-Veda, are hymns to deity—to a number of deities. They were hymns to Indra, the God of Wind and Rain, to Dyaush Pitar, the Jupiter and Zeus Pater of Latins and Greeks, God of the Sky and the Thunder, to Agni, god of fire, and to other gods. That sounds like the animism of early incult races. To an extent that is what it was. For the white men who invaded India from some cradle land in Asia were of the same stock as the Persians, the Greeks, the Romans, the Celts and most of the other forebears of European peoples. And we know how long it was before Europe gave up paganism and polytheism. But in India, a high form of religion came much earlier. Twenty centuries before our era, in the hymns of the Rig-Veda, monotheism, the transcendence of one God, was already asserted.

*Apparent* polytheism is characteristic of India even today. There are countless gods. The greatest of them are Brahma, Vishnu, Shiva, the creator, the preserver, the destroyer. But any educated Indian will tell you that these are merely aspects, names, personifications of the Universal Being. For simple, uneducated people a concept like Brahma, the Absolute, cause of all causes, the One without a second, is too difficult to grasp. Ramakrishna, the great Hindu seer whose influence is reviving and purifying Hinduism even now, was forever worshiping the goddess Kali as his "Divine Mother." Ramakrishna knew that Kali is but an aspect of the One. But the personification to whom his adoration was directed brought a reality to his worship that made him the outstanding saint of nineteenth-century India. But what Hindus, in reply to the charge of idolatry and image worship, insist upon is this: *A Hindu does not worship the image as God, but he worships God through an image.*

The history of a civilization as ancient as that of India is naturally a long one, and can hardly be touched upon here. But when the Aryan invaders pressed farther south from the Indus to the Ganges River, they were opposed by the dark-skinned, earlier inhabitants. The Laws of Manu, a code prescribing every detail of daily life more minutely than the book of Leviticus did for the Hebrews, became the textbook of Hindu living. The caste system arose in an effort to keep the white conquerors and the dark-skinned aborigines, separate. This proved not wholly successful. However, one of the most important of the high castes was that of the Brahmins, to whom alone was reserved the privilege of priesthood. Those priests or Brahmins gradually developed the Brahmanas, a sort of theological literature explaining the religion of the Vedas. The Brahmanas have much to do with ritual, liturgy, sacrifices to the gods and various ideas of rebirth after death. But the really philosophical basis of Hindu religion is to be found in the *Upanishads.*

The Upanishads are called the Vedanta because they are, as it were, the conclusion, the latter end of the Vedas. The word Upanishad means sitting at the feet of, that is, near the teacher of wisdom. There are 108 of the scriptures bearing the name of Upanishad. About ten of them are extremely important. There is no significant form of Hindu thought, it has been said, Buddhism included, "which is not rooted in the Upanishads." They are the great early repository of Indian thought, speculation, philosophy and religion. They were recorded during centuries of time and the best of them are still valid and readable today.

With a lofty inclusiveness, toward which the modern scientific and religious world is still struggling, they proclaim the oneness of all life. The inner immortal self of each one of us and the great cosmic power are one and the same. The world, they insist, is God's revelation of himself. It follows that everything is of Him and in Him, even as the Christian scripture holds that "in Him we live and move and have our being." Indeed, the words of the Upanishad are:

"The Self is one. . . . Unmoving it moves; is far away, yet near; within all, outside all.

**AT BENARES, PIOUS HINDUS** bathe in the holiest of Indian rivers, the Ganges. One of the oldest of world's religious capitals, Benares attracts one million pilgrims yearly to worship in its temples and sacred waters.

↑Meditating in afternoon sun, Hindu priest rests at little shrine near Bombay before proceeding to temple farther up the hill. As devotee of Vishnu the Preserver, he wears vertical white stripes on forehead.

Milling in town square, hundreds of happy Hindus pull huge temple cart with idol on top to Chamundi Hill, Mysore. Brahmans, clinging to sides and pouring coconut milk, lead worship in Dasara "Car" festival. →

Near the end of World War II, 2,000 Hindu priests and tens of thousands of their followers gathered outside New Delhi by sacred river Jumna to pray for world peace. For 10 days, the murmur of their prayers and the smoke of their fires rose like incense from great thatch-and-bamboo pandal (above) built on the plain. For 10 days, austere Brahmans under the leadership of His Holiness Shri Jagadguru chanted a master verse from the 3,000-year-old Vedas: "The sun is the center of the entire universe; all intelligence, all energy, all health are derived from the sun." In all, during this *Mahayajna* or great sacrifice, more than 10,000,000 prayers of praise and supplication were recited. It was probably greatest demonstration of mass praying in modern times, and, as reverent Hindus believe, helped to defeat Axis powers.

"How can a wise man, knowing the unity of life, seeing all creatures in himself, be deluded or sorrowful?

"The Self knows all, is not born, does not die, is not the effect of any cause; is eternal, self-existent, imperishable, ancient.

"When He, the bodiless, leaves the body, exhausts the body, what leaves? That is Self."

The great Self, of which each individual self among us is a part, "cannot be known through discourse, nor found by the mind, or the eye." He that believes in His existence finds Him. How can a man who does not so believe find Him?

The Upanishads, indeed all Indian philosophy and religion, regard it as the supreme imperative task for every man to find Him. But where to look for Him? The Upanishads have an answer for that:

"No eye can see Him, nor has He a face that can be seen, yet through meditation and through discipline He can be found in the heart. He that finds Him enters immortal life." As to this discipline and meditation, it is a deep and fascinating subject. For example, one of the best known of the Upanishads is that of Chandogya, in which a father discusses with his son the knowledge he is supposed to have acquired when he returned from a twelve-year sojourn with his teacher. The father's name was Uddalaka. The son's, Shvetaketu. Like a number of other Upanishads, this is a dialogue.

"My son!" the father began. "You think pretty well of yourself, but did you ask your teacher about the initiation which makes a man hear what is not heard, think what is not thought, know what is not known?"

The father then explained, with a wealth of simile, how in the beginning there was only Being, One without a second, and how that One created out of itself all that is, the many, which inevitably partake of His nature.

"That Being is the seed; all else is but His expression. He is truth, He is Self. Shvetaketu! You are that . . ."

Uddalaka then impressed upon his son that the body bereft of Self dies. But the Self, the Oversoul, the spiritual part of us, does not die. He commanded his son to fetch a banyan fruit.

"Here it is, Lord!" said Shvetaketu.

"Break it," said Uddalaka.

**WHILE MAHARAJAH OF JAIPUR** walks from palace to temple, the faithful experience *darshan* or holy blessing.

Two beautiful *Devadasi* or temple dancers perform a classic Hindu dance amid stone carvings of Mahabalipuram. Young girls, no longer bound by a temple caste, use dance symbolism to express the Divine.

Teen-age Untouchable (below) guards images of god Muniappa on road to Mahabalipuram near Madras. Such an action would have resulted in boy's death until democratic India's recent abolition of slave caste.

One of most famous of Indian temples, Mahabalipuram attracts white-robed Brahmans who admire life-sized elephant cut from solid rock. Thousands of such sages, who live lives of renunciation, purity and prayer, serve their temples and towns and that one Reality which is "Knowledge, Bliss, Existence Absolute." They are India's wise men who know that only ignorance causes men to identify themselves with the body, ego or senses instead of with the universal Spirit. They are the wayside shepherds who tell their followers, "Hear, ye children of immortal bliss! We have known the Ancient One, who is beyond all darkness and delusion. Knowing Him alone you shall be saved from death again and again. He is seen with the eyes of the soul. He is not destroyed when the body is destroyed. He is the Lord of all. He lives in the heart of every being. He, who has become sinless, sees Him, for He enters into that being and becomes one."

Wearing spiked cage which pierces skin repeatedly, Hindu youth in Singapore endures ordeal as soul-purifying discipline. Older Indian (below) in Delhi wears oil-filled containers pinned to his skin. Although not encouraged by either state or temple, such mortifications are still widely practiced in Asia.

"I have broken it, Lord."

"What do you see there?"

"Little seeds, Lord!"

"Break one of them, my son!"

"It is broken, Lord!"

"What do you see there?"

"Nothing, Lord!" said Shvetaketu.

"My son!" said Uddalaka, "this great banyan tree has sprung up from seed so small that you cannot see it. Believe in what I say, my son!

"That Being is the seed; all else but His expression. He is truth. He is Self. Shvetaketu! You are that!"

In brief, the numerous and diverse gods mentioned in the Vedic hymns give way in the Upanishads to the One, the Self, which in the human being is the immortal self. Thus early did the highest Hindu teaching insist that God's dwelling place is the heart of man. The question then arises, How to find Him? Krishna, one of the Avatars, or embodiments of divinity, answers it thus:

"This divine Being, this sublime Friend, is in each of us. God dwells within each man, though few can find Him. This is the path to salvation."

Similarly, Buddha said that "the true nature neither departs nor comes, that it is the same in each of us." A few centuries later, Jesus told his hearers "the kingdom of Heaven is within you."

Much of Krishna's teaching on how to find Him is contained in one of the most beautiful scriptures in the world, the poem called the Bhagavad-Gita, which Sir Edwin Arnold translated into English as "The Song Celestial." This song, or interlude, is part of one of the great epics of India, the *Mahabharata*, recounting some of the legendary wars of the early Hindus. The Bhagavad-Gita is one of the world's favorite classics. In it, Arjuna, one of the warrior princes, is for a time stationary in a kind of no-man's land between the two warring armies, his own and the enemy's. His charioteer is really Krishna the avatar. Arjuna expresses some qualms about killing people, some of them his own kinsmen. Krishna comforts him:

"Thou hast grieved for those who need no grief, and thou speakest words of wisdom! The wise grieve neither for the dead nor for the living.

"For never was I not, nor thou, nor these princes of men; nor shall we ever cease to be in the time to come. . . ." We may recall Emerson's lines based upon this colloquy:

> If the red slayer think he slays,
> Or if the slain think he is slain,

Annual *Ramayana* Festival when Indians celebrate victory of good over evil is most spectacular of ancient ceremonies. Period of pomp and prayer ends with burning in effigy of wicked Ravana by Rama's flaming arrows.

Disciple of Hatayoga, which stresses right eating, exercise, posture, demonstrates fitness to Calcutta crowd. In its higher disciplines of love, detachment and discrimination, Yoga leads aspirant to union with God.

**INDIA'S FOREMOST MODERN SAGE,** Sri Ramana, receives offering of fruit from visiting priests. At top of the holy

hierarchy, he is revered as great Yogi who has broken cycle of rebirths and become one with eternal Brahman.

Performing *Pooja* or worship, penitents bathe at Benares. Here, 100 temples and bath stations line four-mile stretch of Ganges where Shiva passed his mortal days. Pilgrims, beggars and barbers dot station steps.

> They know not well the subtle ways
> I keep, and pass, and turn again.

The Eastern faith in reincarnation is here formulated in the clearest possible terms: "As putting off worn garments, a man takes others new, so putting off worn-out bodies, the lord of the body enters others new. . . . This lord of the body dwells ever immortal in the body of each, O son of Bharata; therefore deign not to grieve even for all beings!"

The belief in reincarnation is an ancient one and by no means confined to India. We in the Occident have learned about it mostly, if not entirely, from Indian literature. No Hindu doubts that after death, after a period of rest and an interval of a sort of spiritual digestion in some other and more subtle world, the human being is born again, and yet again, over and over, until he has worked out his *Karma*. If he improves with every life, grows better, less selfish, more integrated, more spiritual, his Karma also improves. The time will come when he will be led into the path of perfection and ultimately he will be absorbed in Brahman. He "will go no more out."

The word "Karma" means deeds, or works. We receive what we have earned or deserved. Every scripture makes that point. The Christian scrip-

Temple monkeys, revered by Hindus for fabled help of King Rama in epic *Ramayana*, are fed by attendant.

Sacred cows, never slaughtered or milked, roam in streets. In Udaipur, Indian gives cow careful carding.

**PAINTED ELEPHANTS,** caparisoned and mounted for religious parade, are "non-working" by government order.

Annual Palni pilgrimage attracts 200,000 Dravidian peasants to south India town. Here, in worship of Lord Shiva, pilgrims pray, paint their bodies, draw holy "Juggernaut" to hilltop temple (left), gain blessing of high priests like 100-year-old *sadhu* (below). Dravidians, who walk as much as 400 miles on pilgrimage, are dark non-Aryans whose struggles with northern invaders are immortalized in *Ramayana*.

Beloved by 400,000,000 Hindus as the *Mahatma* or Great Soul, Gandhi preached Christlike philosophy of love and nonviolence throughout India. His religious mass movement, resulting in freeing of India from Great Britain, played unique role in shaping modern history.

Eternal, is characteristic of the Way of Knowledge.

Both those ways are good. But *Bhakti Marga,* the way of devotion, is the most popular and the most easily understood. It is the way of love. Being human, we are all moved to prayer, to gratitude, and to devotion. The heart is the great reservoir of religious no less than other emotions. As Krishna, who is Vishnu, who is a personification of Brahma, tells Arjuna:

Cling thou to Me!
Clasp me with heart and mind! so shalt thou dwell
Surely with Me on high. But if thy thought
Droops from such height; if thou be'st weak to set
Body and soul upon Me constantly,
Despair not! give Me lower service! seek
To read Me, worshiping with steadfast will;
And if thou canst not worship steadfastly,
Work for me, toil in works pleasing to Me!

Control, detachment, devotion to the Highest—that is the recipe for union with the Highest.

"The seeker for union, thus ever joining himself in union, his darkness gone, happily attains the infinite joy of union with the Eternal.

"He sees his soul as one with all beings, and all beings as one with his soul, his soul is joined in union, beholding Oneness everywhere."

How lofty are these teachings of the Vedas, the Upanishads, the great Gita! Yet many who have visited India have been surprised to see the villagers and the less educated people everywhere practicing forms of religion remote from those heights, and appearing as frankly polytheistic. Not only every town and village, but virtually every household, seems to have its own favorite deity, to whose image reverence is paid and gift offerings placed. There are many gods specially placated for some particular purpose. Shiva for fertility, Ganesha, the elephant-headed god, for success, Rama for the dying, Yama for the dead. Krishna, Kali, Radha, Hanuman—their number is all but limitless. There are the sacred cows wandering in the streets, receiving almost the reverence of a deity, and the sacred bulls by the roadside. While this is part of the religious tenet of *ahimsa,* harmlessness, that is, harming no living creature, it is a striking phenomenon in Hindu religion and life.

No less so are the pilgrimages to sacred places and shrines and the bathings in sacred rivers. Making pilgrimages to shrines is a trait to which all humanity is more or less susceptible. But the East is peculiarly given to it. The Hajj caravans to Mecca in Mohammedan countries, often at-

ture, in Paul's Epistle to the Galatians, declares in unforgettable words: "Be not deceived; God is not mocked: for whatsoever a man soweth that shall he also reap." That is Karma, and that is the Law. It is inexorable. In India, as we know, the lot of the low castes is hard. The Brahmins and the Kshatriyas were the priests and rulers. The Vaisyas, farmers, merchants and artisans, are still in tolerable fortune. But the Sudras are always servants and some of the very low castes and outcastes are "untouchables." The Hindu attitude was, and is still, that that is their Karma. In the course of cycles of time, they will have worked it out and be born in higher castes. But for Mahatma Gandhi, pious Hindu though he was, that was too much. He worked to have "untouchability" abolished in India.

When Krishna is instructing Arjuna how to reach the heavenly state, he lays down three methods or ways, each of which leads to the goal: the Way of Works, the Way of Knowledge, the Way of Devotion, or Love. The Brahmanas and the Upanishads already taught the first two ways, or yogas. The Way of Devotion is first prominently brought forward in the Bhagavad-Gita. The Way of Works is for anybody who obeys the rules, carries out his duties, observes the rites and ceremonies, is kind and honest and charitable. The Way of Knowledge is the thinker's way, the philosopher's way. The yoga known as Raja Yoga, leading by concentration and meditation to union with the Infinite and

Mohandas Gandhi, India's saintly strategist in long struggle for freedom, chats with friends shortly before 1948 assassination. Although a devout Hindu, Gandhi appreciated beauty of Buddhism, Christianity, Islam.

**FLAME FLICKERS ON GANDHI** pyre at Delhi, as his secretary stares into fire and doctor tries to quiet throng.

Inside temple, Indian family garlands Vaishnavite deity with silks and roses. Amid hundreds of varieties of Hinduism, individual can worship Supreme Brahma as One Infinite Impersonal Spirit or as many gods.

tended by danger and severe hardships and always arduous, is a case in point. In India, to bathe in the Ganges is an achievement of capital importance in the religious life of the populace. It amounts to washing away all one's sins. The broad flights of steps, temple crowned, along the Holy Ganges, are so famous a feature of sacred Benares that they have come to be the pictured symbol of the city.

What do educated Hindus say to all this folk worship, which certainly looks like polytheism, animism, nature-worship, even idolatry? Educated Hindus, still tolerant and always tolerant, would smile with indulgence at our big words. Behind all these multitudes of images, forms, customs and phenomena, there is always Brahma, the Absolute, the One without a second, the source of all and the causeless cause of all. But what of that multiform, heterogeneous worship? It is both a proof and a constant expression of the Hindu's faith in a power greater than himself. It is his innate piety, bred in his bones by countless ages, that moves him to devotion according to his lights. It is emotional religion, to be sure. It is *bhakta*. But few of us are intellectuals or philosophers. Most of us *are* bhaktas. When we feel the need of wor-

Splendidly sculptured, seven-story tower of Mylapore temple dominates Indian countryside. A masterpiece of Dravidian art, the tower is covered with exquisitely carved statues depicting different aspects of the Absolute.

→

Marriage is performed in Bombay according to rites of Brahmo-Samaj, progressive Hindu cult. It teaches individual choice in marriage and belief in personal God. Swastikas around flame are ancient Indian symbols. The

Bhagavad-Gita or "Song of God," India's beloved epic, is chanted to mother and children at home (below) by religious teacher. As widow, she wears white sari but no jewelry. The old guru is supported by temple.

shiping or adoring, or of offering thanks, we pray.

One of the greatest of Hindu bhaktas, and one of the most recent, deserves special attention. He was Ramakrishna, one of the foremost of Indian saints. He died only as recently as 1886, and many people today listen to his immediate disciples at the various Ramakrishna centers in different parts of the world. His favorite disciple, Vivekananda, is still vivid in the memories of many Americans now living. Many had heard him lecture in the United States and many more today are hearing and studying Vedanta as taught by the Swamis at the Ramakrishna centers in the large cities of America.

In any vital religion, there are always movements either toward reform or toward fundamental forms and piety, heresies or reaffirmations. Hinduism has had many such. Buddhism and Jainism themselves, since established as separate religions, were orig-

inally reform movements or heresies. More recently, in the nineteenth century, there arose the Brahmo Samaj, a liberal movement, denouncing the popular polytheism and preaching the underlying basic unity of all religions; and the Arya Samaj, which urges a return to the Vedas, as the purest of all religions. And today, with communism filtering into every Oriental country, materialism is infecting the younger generation.

The Ramakrishna movement, however, seems to have come in advance, as a kind of antidote, at least to communism. In India, there are more than a hundred centers of the Ramakrishna Mission. Some are devoted to the contemplative life, some to social service and education. "The Mission has its own hospitals, dispensaries, high schools," Christopher Isherwood tells us, "industrial and agricultural schools, libraries and publishing houses. In 1941, it opened a college which is affiliated with

**CREMATION BURIAL RITE** is carried out in Calcutta "burning ghat." Ashes of deceased are strewn on Ganges.

the University of Calcutta. It has been consistently active in relieving the victims of earthquakes, floods, famines and epidemics."

Sri Ramakrishna Paramahamsa, as he was called, was born in 1836 of a poor Brahman family in the province of Bengal, and as early as in his twelfth year he was already seeing visions. He became an assistant priest in a temple near Calcutta and a devotee of "the Divine Mother," that is, the goddess Kali. Before long, people came to hear him at the temple of Dakshineswar, to sit at his feet. Almost wholly uneducated himself, he nevertheless attracted educated young men like Vivekananda and a number of others. By many he was recognized as an avatar, a divine incarnation. God may be seen, be known, be taught. It required devotion, devotion and more devotion. Also he taught the underlying harmony, the basic unity of all religions. "Like an inspired prophet he spoke," says the disciple who wrote down his gospel, "and very often he was thrown into a state of Divine Ecstasy! His corporeal frame would become motionless; his respiration stop; his eyes moved not! All sense-consciousness would leave him and he became filled with God-consciousness instead."

Today his disciples, the Swamis of the Ramakrishna Order, are teaching his gospel everywhere. In the United States alone, there are eleven centers and they teach Vedanta, Yoga, the wisdom of the Upanishads and the Bhagavad-Gita. Such intellectuals as Aldous Huxley, Gerald Heard, Christopher Isherwood and the playwright, John van Druten, are helping to promote the movement. Hinduism, which unlike Buddhism was not reckoned as a world religion, but rather as a national one, is now spreading out beyond its own borders, carrying the irrepressible teaching of the absolute One.

In the words of Ralph Waldo Emerson's Brahma:

> They reckon ill who leave me out;
>   When me they fly I am the wings;
>   I am the doubter and the doubt.

Ramakrishna's creed, expressed at its briefest, also sums up the Vedanta philosophy: "The many religions are so many paths to God."

Handsome old *sadhu* is typical of holy men who wander about India praying, fasting, blessing people with their purifying presence. Healer (above), who lives near sacred Mt. Arunchala in Tiruvannamalai, specializes in increasing fertility in childless wives. His worldly needs are negligible, and rice ration is delivered daily to his retreat by faithful disciples.

On Mysore hilltop, another holy man meditates before stone statue 2,000 years old. Worshiping Brahma the Creator and beholding the One in all things, thousands of such *sadhus* make Hinduism a living reality for 400 million believers. Devout Hindus avow that through prayer, devotion and dedicated work, all souls finally attain to perfect union with the Supreme Spirit.

→

# 2. BUDDHISM

## *Four noble truths and the eightfold Path to Nirvana*

BUDDHISM, LIKE EVERY GREAT RELIgion, is a romance of the human spirit. It is a daring plunge into the Unknown for the purpose of bringing back to the human race that knowledge which is life itself.

Today there are said to be 150,000,000 Buddhists in Asia. But we really cannot be sure of the numbers. The population of China is variously estimated at 400 to 500 millions. Much of that population, at least 250 million, practices, at one and the same time, the three religions of Taoism, Confucianism and Buddhism. Are the 150 million believers of the reference books people for whom Buddhism is the only religion? We simply do not know. But we do know that even to us Occidentals, accustomed to weigh and measure and classify everything, Buddhism is one of the greatest religious philosophies on earth.

A modern intellect and historian, the late H. G. Wells, had this to say on Buddhism: "The fundamental teaching of Gautama, as it is now being made plain to us by the study of original sources, is clear and simple and in the closest harmony with modern ideas. It is beyond all dispute the achievement of one of the most penetrating intelligences the world has ever known."

The world is a big place with a long history. If the author of Buddhism was one of the most penetrating intelligences the world has ever known, we in our turn cannot learn too much about him. Who was he? What did he discover? How was his intelligence directed? Fortunately, though he lived a long time ago, we know a great deal about him.

He was a prince in northern India, born in 560 B.C., heir to a rajah's throne. And though his father's kingdom was small, the son nevertheless lived in great luxury, cushioned against the shocks or even the merely unpleasant things of life. One habit he possessed, not often associated with young princes,

Buddhist pilgrim, approaching Gyangtse in Tibet to celebrate joyous festival of Wesak, looks out over city's cluster of sacred temples including famous circular Kum-Bum Pagoda (center). Buddhism, which

stresses man's destiny as eternal enlightenment, urges disciplines of long pilgrimages as means to merit and inner peace. Prince Siddhartha, who became the *Buddha* or Enlightened One, preached selflessness, non-violence, and purity of thought, told his followers to "be diligent and energetic, and live in the world not a life of self but a life of truth. Then, surely, joy, peace and bliss will dwell in your minds."

Japanese sage sits in lotus posture as he ponders virtues of charity, piety, self-control. Priest is member of Zen sect which stresses meditation as way to transcendental wisdom. U. S. Buddhist (below) reads sacred Buddhist scriptures, the Sutta-Nipata.

Buddha's
Four Noble Truths

The truth of Suffering
The truth of the cause of suffering
The truth of the cessation of suffering
The truth of the way to end suffering
by treading the noble eight fold path

The Eight Fold Path

Right ideas · Right recollectiveness
Right effort · Right mindfulness
Right behavior · Right meditation
Right vocation · Right resolution

四聖諦
苦聖諦
集聖諦
滅聖諦
道聖諦

八正道
正思惟
正語
正業
正命
正精進
正念
正中道

was the habit of thoughtfulness. This caused his father much concern. An heir apparent to a throne should be cheerful, carefree, jovial and healthy. He shouldn't bother too much about the deeper problems of life. But Prince Siddhartha Gautama was rather different. Notwithstanding all his pleasures and distractions, he perceived the basic flaws of life and these bit deeply into his consciousness.

Sickness, old age, death! What a trinity for man, the noblest creature that walks the earth, to be subject to! None can escape those grim executioners, be he prince or pauper, gentle or simple, rich or lowly—none can escape. What could the human race be about, to remain so negligent, to take no measures to wipe out those enemies, to annihilate them? Could they be annihilated? That, too, required thought. And there was nothing on earth that more urgently called for thought. Where could he do this thinking, this concentrated meditation? In his father's court, surrounded by sycophants and dancing girls, anxious to please and amuse him? Clearly that was out of the question.

So, in the time-honored narrative of the Buddha's life, we come upon this dramatic scene: the young prince, aged twenty-nine, is stealing in the night toward his young wife's bedchamber. She and his infant son are lying asleep there, and he tiptoes to the bed to take a last look at them. He dares not touch either for fear of waking them. That might interfere with his purpose which is now fixed and decided. He would go forth into the world, to what holy men and ascetics in his country called the homeless life, to try to solve the problem of human misery.

Is there any way to escape from the human scourges of sickness, old age and death? The answer to that is what he must set himself to seek. He leaped upon his horse Kanthaka, accompanied only by his charioteer, Channa, rode out of the palace gates and left his native city, Kapilavastu, behind him. After traveling a certain distance, he changed his garments, donned the yellow robe of the ascetic, and lost himself in the immemorial roads and by-paths of India.

He had taken the great step. The prince Siddhartha Gautama was now one of the countless thousands of homeless wanderers, seekers, as they say, after truth. In India, there is no disgrace in being a mendicant, provided one is a mendicant in a holy cause, a seeker of the truths by which saints and holy men live and teach others to live. Who would not help with a

Passing dragons guarding entrance to Shwe Dagon Pagoda, Buddhist nuns return to Rangoon cloisters. Young Sisters, who visit temple twice a month, shave their heads, wear white-and-yellow robes, lead devotional lives of prayer and contemplation. Unlike most Christian nuns, they keep aloof from world.

Burmese women rest on temple floor after praying before biggest Buddha in Burma. Located in Rangoon's Kemmendine Monastery and covered with iron shed, 40-foot statue depicts Buddha in state of bliss. Rangoon, one of Orient's truly fairy-tale cities, is filled with yellow-robed priests and golden shrines such as Shwe Dagon (right). Its serenity is rooted in its religion and all things in Rangoon—the temples, bells, people and priests—combine to honor the Lord Buddha. Buddhism itself, extending from Mongolia to the Pacific and from Arctic to Indian Ocean, is followed by one tenth of world's peoples.

Mi Lei Fo or Laughing Buddha, part of 1,400-year-old sculptures lining approaches to Ling Ying Monastery near

Burmese worshippers leave Rangoon's great golden Shwe Dagon Pagoda, after celebrating Thadingyut Festival marking end of the rainy season. Soaring shrine, which measures 375 feet in height and 1,355 feet in circumference, is covered with gold leaf applied layer on layer by pious Buddhists. Built upon a hill and dominating the city, Shwe Dagon is surrounded by scores of smaller temples housing hundreds of Buddhas. Bits of glass, pottery and precious stones sparkle from the multicolored towers. The pungent smell of incense fills the air. Flowers, brought daily by Burmese pilgrims, decorate every temple.

Hangchow, draws tourists and faithful for picture taking. Colorful Chinese monastery is known as "Soul's Retreat."

In deep meditation, Buddhist students sit rigidly in Japan's centuries-old Zen temple at Kamakura. Watchful monk (left above) raps any novice caught napping while pondering problems posed by temple's Abbott Asahina (left below). Six times monthly, priests shave each other's pates (below). Zennists, who are spiritual descendants of Indian seer Daruma Daishi, spend six hours daily concentrating mind upon the Absolute.

little food, a bit of rice, cooked vegetables, or what not, to one who has left everything behind to seek for the true way of life on earth?

In India, particularly in the religious life, the *guru* principle is very strong. Guru means teacher. Every novice has a teacher, and every teacher has a higher teacher to whom he in turn looks for guidance. Prince Gautama, having assumed the homeless life of the ascetic, attached himself first to one teacher, then to another. What they had to impart had nothing new in it for him. He moved on. Nor did the austerities practiced by so many of India's ascetics seduce this princely seeker. He could see no profit to the Creator of all things when, as he put it, "the bones of my spine when bent and straightened were like a row of spindles through the little food. As the beams of an old shed stick out, so did my ribs stick out through the little food."

"If one could attain perfection," he said, "and liberation from the bonds which tie man to the earth only through the renunciation of food and human conditions, then a horse or a cow would have reached it long since."

That kind of talk did not endear him to those steeped in the long Indian tradition of asceticism, and those near him drew away from him. Left alone and solitary, while sitting rapt in meditation under a great banyan known since as the Bodhi tree, he had a series of tremendous spiritual experiences that brought him Illumination, Enlightenment. He now knew, he felt, how to put an end to human suffering. He called his method the Middle Way, since it renounced luxury and satiety upon the one hand and mere flagellant asceticism upon the other.

Exactly what is it that Gautama, henceforth called the Buddha, discovered in his Enlightenment? As a philosophy of life it seems so simple, one almost hesitates to write it down. The Four Noble Truths of suffering are simply these: 1. Existence is suffering. 2. Suffering is caused by desire or attachment to life and the things of this life. 3. To conquer suffering a human being must annihilate the craving of desire and attachment to life.

So far we have only three Noble Truths. No one will think they are easy. To annihilate desire in this world is no task for babes. The Buddha, of course, was aware of that. His program for bringing it about is contained in the Fourth Noble Truth: to attain cessation of clinging, or attachment, one must follow the Noble Eightfold Path. The eight rules of this path are, if anything, even simpler than the Four Truths. They are: right belief, right aims, right speech, right actions, right occupation, right endeavor, right mindfulness or thinking, right medi-

Before presenting himself as candidate for discipleship, Zen novitiate humbles himself in outer court. Upon acceptance, he begins life of prayer and work in fields.

Austere program, starting with 4 A.M. breakfast and ending with 8 P.M. retirement, trains Buddhist for loving service and luminous consciousness of Nirvana.

Borobudur Monument, built in 9th century and located 90 miles north of Indonesian capital of Jogjakarta, is largest Buddhist temple in the world. The massive pile, consisting of nine ornamented stories and central cupola, stands 128 feet high and measures 500x500 feet at the base. Borobudur, which means "monastery on a hill," was part of Renaissance-like flowering of art and architecture inspired by spread of Buddhism beyond borders of India. Constructed as a burial place for the ashes of Gautama and containing 2,000 images and bas-reliefs depicting historical Buddha's struggle for liberation, great temple is one of most beautifully decorated shrines on earth.

atheist and Buddhism as atheistical. But when faced squarely with the question as to an ultimate divine reality, Buddha replied:

"There is an unborn, an unoriginated, an uncompounded; were there not, O mendicants, there would be no escape from the world of the born, the originated, the made and the compounded."

His Eightfold Path sounds less like a system of religion than like a set of rules laid down by some profound modern psychologist. Live rightly, it seems to say, and your future is assured, to say nothing of the present. Infringe upon these rules and you will inevitably pay and go on paying until you learn better. The payment is in only one coin—suffering.

His first converts were five ascetics who had reviled him for giving up asceticism and taking the Middle Way. He found those ascetics again in the Deer Park at Sarnath, near Benares. But now, now that he had achieved Enlightenment, they could not choose but listen to him. He was no longer like themselves, a mere seeking wanderer. He spoke now with the authority of one who had found, who had attained. That was the beginning of his ministry. For some forty-five years he wandered up and down India, with an increasing following, teaching and

Child *Bodhisattvas* or "beings destined for Enlightenment" inspire adult reverence throughout Buddhist world. Burma boy (right), pensive in prayer in Rangoon monastery, is learning eightfold Middle Path of Lord Buddha—right views, right resolve, right speech, right behavior, right livelihood, right effort, right mindfulness, right meditation—which lead to extinction of suffering and selfless joys of Nirvana. Tibetan teen-ager (above) is representative of perfect beings, who, as northern Buddhists believe, are born again to help others attain Enlightenment. Seated on cushioned throne in Dug-Kar monastery, he mirrors in his tranquil gaze the conviction of his divinity and sacred mission to save mankind. Little Chinese boys (left) leave Hangchow's magnificent Yeo Fei Temple, after participating in Buddhist service. Dressed in blue silk coats, orange pants and headdresses topped with red balls and carrying Buddhist icons, youngsters had taken part in religious processional from Hangchow to Yeo Fei five miles away. Temple itself was built 300 years ago to honor 12th century Chinese general and Buddha the Merciful.

tation. The key to the Buddhist is the word "right."

Where is the theology, where the dialectics, the arguments, the Hells and the Heavens, the pictures of a future life? The Buddha never dealt in such things. It was his belief that there was no profit in discussing them, considering all that there is for us to do in our brief and troubled earthly life. That is one reason some have described Buddha as an

At halfway mark in flight from Lhasa, Dalai Lama's party approaches fortress town of Gyangtse. Boy king rides in sedan chair, as ceremonial dancers greet him (right). Small stones along route ward off evil spirits.

1,000 room, 300-year-old palace is home of Dalai Lama, Tibet's "Living Buddha." When Chinese Reds invaded country, 15-year-old god-king made 284-mile journey (left) from Lhasa to Yatung, near Indian border. Dalai Lama (below) receives relics of original Gautama Buddha brought from India for his veneration. Holding gold urn is Chi-khyap Khem-po, Lord Chamberlain of Tibet. Young king has returned to mountain capital.

45

Rangoon's Reclining Buddha (above) is center of Taz-aungdine monastery of 200 monks. Immense statue, called Baya-Gyi, measures 70 by 181 feet. Peiping's smiling Buddha (below) is in prayer hall of great Yung Ho Kung Temple. Ancient capital's monuments reflect both Buddhist serenity and Confucian learning.

preaching his simple, but profound, philosophy:

There are four motive forces or powers that lead us into evil doing and evil living. They are desire, hatred, delusion and fear. Extirpate, by every means in our power, greed, lust, hate and fear, and even on earth life approaches paradise. What need to picture imaginary heavens in space?

There are said to exist some ten thousand Buddhist scriptures. We may be sure Buddha did not write them. So far as we know, he did not write anything. Like most great religious teachers, he talked to his disciples and to groups of hearers. He was forever telling them the simple truths that make up the bases of all the great religions. Enough to expound the Eightfold Path. "All that we are," he said, "is the result of what we have thought. If a man speaks or acts with an evil thought, pain follows him, as the wheel follows the foot of the ox that draws the wagon. . . . If a man speaks or acts with a pure thought, happiness follows him, like a shadow that never leaves him." Do we not know of another Scripture that tells us, "As a man thinketh in his heart, so is he"?

"He who destroys life, who speaks untruth, who in this world takes what is not given him, who goes to another man's wife, even in this world, digs up his own root.

"There is no fire like lust, there is no spark like hatred, there is no snare like folly, there is no torrent like greed.

"Let us live happily then, not hating those who hate us! Among men who hate us, let us dwell free from hatred!"

These sayings and many others like them appear in Buddha's *Dhammapada,* or Path of Wisdom. Needless to say, he did not collect them. He only said them, in his various sermons and discourses. They were collected much later by some of his disciples and written down. That is also true of many of the Buddhist scriptures. But by far the greater number were not uttered by him, but were merely based on disciples' interpretations of his utterances. That is the way theologies arise.

First of all there came into being the two great divisions of Buddhism, the Hinayana and the Mahayana. The Hinayana, which literally means the smaller vehicle, consists chiefly in the simple teachings of Buddha after he attained Enlightenment. There is hardly any theology in it. Today that kind of Buddhism is found in Ceylon, Siam and Burma.

Mahayana, however, which means the great vehicle, is pretty much the Buddhism of the rest of the Buddhist world. It is the Buddhism of Tibet, of China, of Japan, of Mongolia. It is the Buddhism of the different sects. For, as in all great religions, sects are numerous in Buddhism.

If, for instance, you were to see Buddhist religion practiced in Burma and then in Tibet, with its prayer wheels, you could easily believe you were seeing the practice of two different religions. The Burmese monk, an intimate member of the community, reading some simple passage of scripture to people out of doors near the monastery, or instructing children, represents one kind of Buddhism. The monks in their gorgeous vestments in, say, the Lama Temple of Peiping, with its atmosphere of high ritual and wealth, appear very remote from the simpler Hinayana form. In Japan alone, there are numerous sects. There is the Shingon, the Tientai, the Nichiren, the Pure Land sect, and there is the Zen sect, which began in China and developed there and in Japan.

The word *Zen* is the Japanese way of pronouncing the word *Channa*, which in turn is the Chinese way of pronouncing the Sanskrit word *dhyana*. The word means meditation. Now, we know that meditation is characteristic of oriental religions, much as prayer is characteristic of Christianity. Why then this special designation of a Buddhist sect as Zen, which really means meditation?

The reason brings us a fascinating glimpse into oriental psychology. It is true that Buddhism, like Hinduism, Jainism, Vedanta, demands the practice of meditation. The Chinese, however, are an exceedingly practical people. Buddhism came to them from India first in pre-Christian times and again in the first century and in the sixth century, A.D. The usual subjects of Buddhist meditation are such things as the virtues, love, compassion, charity, the transitoriness of human life, the repulsive aspects of death. To the pious Buddhist in India, it didn't matter if he did not get very far in this life. He had numerous incarnations before him in the future in which to perfect himself. To the Chinese Buddhist, that seemed too slow a process. He wanted to achieve Nirvana, or Enlightenment, not in some remote future life, but now, soon, in his present life.

One of the Hindu missionaries, who came to China in the sixth century, had the method that exactly suited the Chinese temperament. His name was Bodhidarma. His message included four cardinal points:

A special transmission outside the scriptures;
No dependence upon words and letters;
Direct pointing at the soul of man;
Seeing into one's own nature and attainment of Buddahood.

This was revolutionary. "No dependence upon

In Buddhism's 2,500-year surge across Asia, statues to founder assumed characteristics of countries it invaded. Slimmer alabaster Buddha (above) occupies 30-foot niche in Colombo pagoda in Ceylon. Kamakura's Great Buddha (below), cast in bronze in 1252 and standing 49 feet high, is most majestic monument in Japan.

Saffron-robed priests surround crocodile pool on old temple grounds of Wat Po in Bangkok, Thailand. Lancelike spires are part of 400 temples which make Bangkok a monument to Lord Buddha and most impressive Buddhist capital.

Dances of devotion, like all arts dedicated to Buddha, show classical oriental influence. Richly costumed Shwe-Man-Tin Maung dancers perform on Burma holiday.

Parade of little girls, shepherded by mothers and taking place in Tokyo, commemorates opening of Buddhist shrine. Ornate kimonos recall Japan's ancient queens.

Prince Thondup Nangyol, son of Maharaja of Sikkim, marries Princess Sangey Deki, kinswoman of 7th Dalai Lama of Tibet, in ceremony at Gangtok. Symbolically, tables are piled high with food. Sikkim nobles (below) ride to wedding through 14,000-foot pass in Himalayas.

words and letters"—that practically puts piety and ritualism into the background. But seeing into one's own nature—that was the very heart of the new program. It meant not merely waiting for Enlightenment as some far-off divine event, but doing something about it as actively as possible. Enlightenment, what we now call religious experience, usually comes in a flash of intuition that reassures us, integrates our whole being, makes us feel secure and at one with creation. The Zen Buddhists of China decided not merely to wait for this experience, but to promote it, in a sense to compel it, by a special technique they worked out. The technique consisted largely in the *koan*, and the practice of *zazen*.

The koan is simply a problem set by the master for the student to meditate on. But it is like no problem we ever meet in any logical field or context. It is designed to heighten and develop the intuitive faculty of the disciple until he reaches the particular saturation point that will suddenly bring him the flash of intuition that changes his outlook on life. The result is called *satori*, or Enlightenment. And to be enlightened is to be one with Buddha, indeed, with all the Universe, with all that is.

There are said to be some eighteen hundred such koans, or problems, upon which the disciple progressively meditates until he attains satori. Lists of the koans exist, but there are no answers in the back of the book. Only the master can attest whether or not the disciple has gained satori, or whether he must go on trying in the meditation hall, and continue the practice of zazen. One of the favorite first koans generally assigned to the student is this: What was your original face before your parents were born?

Obviously no logical answer to this query is possible. But to the Buddhist steeped in monism, in the belief in the all-inclusive oneness of life, in the principle that our true nature neither departs nor comes, but is always present, albeit beclouded by external objects, to such a one, after due process of meditation, an answer is possible. True, the correct answer may be some action or gesture rather than so many words. But there is a right answer for every koan. Some well-known koans are such as these:

All things return to the One. Where does the One return?

Who is it that carries about this corpse of yours?
Has a dog Buddha-nature?
When I pass over the bridge the water flows not, but the bridge flows.

Clearly, no logical answers are possible to any of

Wedding's daylong feasting is climaxed by four-hour ceremonial dance performed by masked Lamas and led by Tibetan trumpeters (above) with 10-foot horns. After the ceremony, which was performed to chanting of prayers and playing of Lama band, both royal and common guests gathered on palace grounds to consume trays of food and tea. The marriage, like all traditional unions between Sikkim and Tibetan ruling houses, was arranged by intermediaries, and bride and groom did not glimpse each other until their wedding day.

these problems, not any more than to the famous koan: Two hands when clapped produce a certain sound. What is the sound of one hand clapping? The attempt to hear the sound of one hand *can* transport one into the realm of the Absolute, the One, where there are no relations or distinctions, no multiplicity or diversity, only unity. That is the design and aim of all the koans, to make the intuition grow, to cast out prejudices, to merge the individual consciousness in the Universal. But where, some may ask, is the *religion* in that? The chief aim to a Buddhist is to be able to get rid of the personal self, the self-centered life, and live only the self-less life. And is not that the true aim of every great religion? The goal of the Buddhist is the good life, perfection. And the greatest virtue of all, Buddha taught, was the *loving heart*.

Throughout the rainy season of India, Buddha, with his disciples and followers gathered about him in a park or building, would hold discourse, answer questions, expound his doctrine and, in short, teach. But once the rainy season was over, he would send his monks to far places to carry the messages of the good life, the Middle Way. He himself would take to the road and, begging bowl in hand, with downcast eyes, he would pause at doorways like any other mendicant friar, receiving what was given, but asking for nothing. Once, it is related, he came to his

Standing row on row in a forest of scepters and halos, 1,001 gilded statues of Kwannon, Buddhist goddess of mercy line two sides of Temple of Sanusan-gen-do in Kyoto. Built in 1266, seven centuries after Buddhism was brought to Japan from China, the temple signifies Buddha's boundless compassion to Japan's 45 million believers. The many hands of "thousand-armed" goddess suggest she has countless weapons. The lotus which she holds symbolizes heavenly purity. The axes and arrows, clasped in her remaining hands, warn devotees that Kwannon can be fierce when patience is exhausted.

father's realm, where the king, now resigned to his son's vocation, together with the populace, awaited the "return of a glorious teacher" to their clan. When the king saw the yellow-robed monk with the begging bowl, pausing at doorways, and recognized his own son, he could not bear it. He hurried to him and told him he was disgracing a royal family.

"It is our custom, O King," said the Enlightened One.

"No one of our royal lineage ever begged," said the king, with all the bitterness of a father deeply disappointed in his son.

"That royal lineage is your lineage, O King," said the Tathagata, he who had thus come. "Mine is the Buddha lineage."

That was beyond this normal father's understanding. He took the begging bowl out of his son's hand, a custom well understood by Hindus, which means "while you are with me all your wants will be supplied," and led him to the palace. All the people came to do him reverence, all excepting Yashodara, the wife he had left behind him years earlier.

"If the mother of his son has any value in his eyes," she said, "he will come to me." This of course he did. He was too noble to do otherwise. Their meeting was dramatic. His own consciousness, while full of kindness and compassion, was now beyond the ordinary emotions of men. Yashodara could not at first understand his tranquil look. Then she ran toward him and threw herself at his feet, weeping bitterly. Subsequently both she and their son, Rahula, joined branches of his Order of Monks and nuns.

For forty-five years after his Enlightenment, the Buddha thus went about India preaching and teaching his doctrine, namely, that the only way to get rid of suffering is to follow the Eightfold Path, to rid oneself of the craving for life. That alone will put an end to rebirth. To be born is to suffer. To cease being born is salvation, Nirvana.

He died in his eightieth year from eating a dish, it is said, which, though distasteful to him, he was too courteous to his host to decline. His monks and near disciples gathered about him, some of them weeping piteously when he told them he was about to die. He tried to comfort them with some of his basic teachings: that all the visible universe is transient, that all component things must eventually fall apart, since transiency is inherent in them. His last words were: "Monks, be ye lamps unto yourselves. Work out your own salvation with diligence."

Sitting before great golden effigy of their Lord, Rangoon Buddhists pray, chant and eat noodles in observance of Fire Festival marking end of monsoon and start of sunny winter. They are a few of the millions in a

dozen countries who accept teachings of Indian prince born 500 years before Christ. Following renouncing of his kingdom and gaining of Enlightenment, Buddha taught Four Noble Truths of prevalence of sorrow, and Eightfold Path leading to its extinction. Buddhists, following Middle Way and striving to overcome sense of "I," ignorance and ill-will, combine morality and precise meditation as means to Buddhahood or ultimately Real.

China's ancient walled city of Peiping has been capital of Confucianism as well as Chinese art and culture for 2,000 years. Splendid archway (above), on Imperial Pleasure Island near the city, leads up stairway to famous White Pagoda built by Ming emperors in 15th century. Confucianism, which has been both symbol and model of the Chinese for nearly twenty-five centuries, is known in the Orient as "the teachings of the scholar." Confucius considered *Li* or propriety as a central principle unifying his thought. When a disciple asked for a one-word guide to life, the Teacher replied, "Is not reciprocity such a word?"

# 3. CONFUCIANISM

*Only order, reverence, reciprocity can produce "Superior Man"*

CONFUCIANISM IS PERHAPS THE best illustration of the truth that supernatural religious experiences are not necessarily indispensable to the founding of a great religion.

For Confucius himself, Master Kung, as he was called, was not in the strict sense of the word a religious man at all. He was not a prophet, not even so far as we know, a mystic. He claimed no revelation from Heaven. He was only a good and a wise man. Yet his temples exist throughout China even today, and communism there will have a hard time uprooting his cult. Indeed, communism may yet break on the rock of Confucianism. For Confucianism is not so much a creed as it is a way of life. And so deeply is it ingrained in Chinese mores, ethics, customs and beliefs, no one who knows China can imagine it wholly extirpated.

People speak of this or that hero or great man leaving his "stamp" upon a people. It is safe to say that no man more thoroughly left his stamp upon a nation than did Confucius upon the Chinese. Yet such was his modesty that on one occasion he said, "I was not born a wise man. I am merely one who is in love with ancient studies and works very hard to learn them." To such an extent did he study the ancient wisdom, the ancient classics, the decaying remnants of the ancient religion, that not only the "superior man," but even the veriest coolie showed some of the traits, at least in respect for his elders, of the cultivated gentleman. Confucius was so great a teacher that reverence for him became a religion for four hundred million people.

The ancient Chinese religion, with its spirit worship, and its sacrifices, was really a kind of animism. Ancestor worship is much older than Confucius. But whatever there had been in the ancient religion that was good, Confucius brought forward, renovated, as it were, gave it the impress of his personality and made it live. He was not a maker, a creator, he quite frankly admitted, but "a transmitter," a hander-on.

Some writers compare him to England's Dr. Samuel Johnson. A monument of personality he certainly was, but on a vastly greater scale than Johnson. He seemed to be always preoccupied with the virtues and always with the problem of perfect, or at least ideal, conduct and government of states. He became one of the greatest personalities in history. "The Perfect Sage" one emperor called him (after his death), and posthumous titles of no-

Confucius, China's Great Sage and greatest moral teacher, set an entire society's code of conduct with his "Silver Rule," "What you do not like done to yourself, do not do to others."

Chinese religious exuberance and artistic imagination decorated temples with lavish sculptures and carvings. God of Fire (above) wards off evil spirits in Temple of 10,000 Buddhas in Western Hills, while God of Fury (below) guards Confucian shrine in Kunming.

bility were conferred upon him. But, as is the way with human nature, his contemporaries, though praising him, also laughed at him. They extolled his virtues, but wanted them at a distance. For a brief time, he held office in the government of a state. When that was over, he wandered about China for thirteen years, hoping some other prince would employ him. No one did. Yet to subsequent generations of Chinese, that homeless wanderer became little short of a God.

Though he was born twenty-five centuries ago, in 551 B.C., much is known of Confucius and his family, because of the great reverence paid him by all Chinese. He was a descendant of the Sung family, a line of dukes who ruled the eastern part of Honan until the dukedom lapsed. The family then took the name of Kung, which is still the greatest name in China. For political reasons this family migrated to the state of Lu and there Confucius was born.

His father, Shuh-liang Ho, was by trade a soldier, with an honorable career of service. He was a powerful man physically, but, though the father of nine daughters, he had no son who would perform the necessary rites and religious functions at and after his death. In China, that was a tragic matter. So, though over seventy, Shuh-liang married again, and the young wife, Ching-tsai, bore him the son whom all China came to reverence and adore.

In the case of all great heroes, particularly religious leaders, clusters of legends accumulate about their birth. It is as though mankind cannot believe that in itself lie the potentialities for the greatest heights. The answer to Ching-tsai's prayer for a son brought the assurance, by a spirit: "You shall have a son beyond other men." A dream showed her a mythical animal, perhaps it was a unicorn, which spat out a tablet, reading: "Thy son shall be a throneless king." In due course the son was born, and of his boyhood as little is known as is the case with most great men. We do know, however, that his father's death occurred when the boy was three, that his young mother saw to it that he obtained a good education, and that he early helped out in the family livelihood.

"When I was young," he later said, "my condition was low, and so I gained ability in many things."

He was only seventeen when he received an appointment in the state of Lu as tithe collector for one of the three ruling families of the state. A tenth of the produce, in the form of grain, of

Lighting prayer candle in Hangchow temple, worshiping widow pays tribute to spirit of dead husband. Confucianism, which became synonymous with Chinese culture, adopted practice of ancestor worship from the first.

Hongkong family in mourning white kneel as body of son is placed aboard launch for burial on mainland.

Dragon Festival Day, which occurs on "first day of second moon of spring," is celebrated in Nanking with parades, rickshaw rides, rites in the Fu-Tso Miao Temple.

By old Manchu Decree, there must be Temple of Confucius in every town. Rites of Confucianism, now largely an act of reverence, are performed by civil leaders.

every farm, went to the Duke. To collect that grain was Confucius' first employment. "My calculations must all be right," he said. "That is what I have to care about." We may be sure that they were right, that he was a model official, and very soon his reputation was such that two sons of one of the ruling families of Lu came to study under him. He married at the age of nineteen, was father of a son at twenty and was sufficiently prominent to receive a present of fish from the Duke to celebrate his son's birth.

In no religious sense, and not even in the strict academic sense, he became a teacher famous far beyond the borders of his own state. His teaching, carried on in his own home, made a sort of university of morals, politics, government and philosophy. When we say that Mark Hopkins on one end of a log and a student on the other constituted a college, we infer an education in the sense that

Confucius gave one to his disciples. It was personal, individual and lofty, a combination of precept and example. The specific subjects of instruction, history, government, poetry, music, propriety and divination, were the rubrics of the curriculum. But more important than any of these was the character and personality of the teacher. Dr. Samuel Johnson's influence made a man of a rather unimportant little Scotsman called Boswell. The teaching and influence of Confucius created a group of scholars, philosophers, statesmen and high government officials in a number of Chinese states. More than that, his influence has survived twenty-four centuries. The temples devoted to his worship still dot the land of China, and his name is as famous as that of any teacher of mankind with the possible exception of Jesus of Nazareth.

What was the teaching of this "uncrowned king of China"? To begin with, we have his own words

Classically beautiful *Pailou* or heavenly gate of Peiping's Summer Palace shows Chinese striving for spiritual values in secular as well as religious architecture.

Located in Purple Forbidden City, the Palace Park is filled with elaborately decorated pavilions and pagodas dedicated both to Confucius and Buddha.

that "a central thread" runs through all his knowledge and teaching. That connecting and unifying thread is *reciprocity*. Of the true, or superior, man he said: "What he does not want done unto himself, he does not do unto others." That Golden Rule, which we find in every scripture of every great religion, is almost a scripture in itself. But notwithstanding its brevity, mankind has thus far found it impossible to learn. When we do learn it, most of our troubles will end.

We hear and speak of the Five Classics of Confucius as though he were their author and had composed every word of them. Present-day scholarship holds otherwise. The Classics already existed when Confucius came upon the scene. As he said, "I am a transmitter, not a creator." It is his comments and interpretations that expressed his philosophy and form the basis of his fame. The book known as the *Analects* of Confucius is a mine of

his sayings, a sort of compendium or Bible. The sayings are mostly detached, torn from their context, brief, but sufficiently pithy to rank as wisdom through the ages, as for instance:

"A man who has committed a mistake and doesn't correct it is committing another."

"It is easy to be rich and not proud; it is hard to be poor and not complain."

"Goody-goody people are the thieves of virtue."

The Confucian Classics include the Book of History or *Shu Ching*, the Book of Poetry, or *Shih Ching*, *Li Chi*, or the Book of Rites, *I Ching*, or the Book of Changes, and the Annals of Spring and Autumn, or *Ch'un Ch'iu*. Ever since Confucius' death, scholars have been debating, arguing and speculating as to how much of those works was from the master's own hands, how much was contributed by his original disciples, how much by later disciples and what portions were handed on

World-famous *T'ien T'an* or Temple of Heaven (above) is the most sacred edifice in all China. Here, in triple-roofed, lavishly colored prayer hall, Ming and Manchu emperors worshiped before Confucian "tablets of Heaven" and here today commoners still pray for peace, health and plentiful harvests. Temple, which is part of the Altar of Heaven in Peiping's South City and which is faced by similar blue-roofed Temple of the God of the Universe, has its doors, windows and gates facing south according to tradition. Statues and tablets honoring Father of Chinese culture and his disciples are maintained here and in similar temples throughout the country. Temple ceremonies honoring Confucius are never religious, for Chinese worship their Sage not as a god but as a great teacher and pattern of prestige. Similarly, Nanking's striking Memorial Pagoda (far left) and Hangchow's storied Moon God Shrine typify thousands of sacred structures commemorating not only Master Kung but China's other prophets, statesmen, poets and war heroes. Multi-tiered pagodas usually are covered with carvings showing scenes from Confucian and Buddhist mythology.

from antiquity without change. It is certain that the *Shih-Ching,* the Book of Poetry, or "Odes," comes from antiquity. It contains some of the most beautiful poetry China has produced. The most characteristic of the Classics is the *Li Chi,* or Book of Rites. It is a sort of glorified book of etiquette. But let us not make the mistake of thinking that it is merely an old Chinese Emily Post. The *Li* is really a bible of conduct in all departments of life.

China's modern sage, Lin Yutang, makes a genuine contribution to the understanding of Confucius by pointing out that he identifies politics with ethics. Even a moment's reflection on what it would mean for any society, including our own, if politics were conducted on the highest ethical levels, elevates Confucius to the company of mankind's greatest teachers. Government, to him, was a way, an effort to "put things in order." To him, certainly, order was Heaven's first law. But the opening line of his Book of Rites is: "Always and in everything let there be reverence." It was conduct he stressed, conduct in everything, in government, in marriage, in parenthood, in sonship, in all human relationships. Order and reverence,

For centuries, in every Chinese home, children learned maxims of Confucius from temple scholars. Even today, as in Chungking home (above), reading of such Confucian classics as *The Analects* is preparation for life in the world or devotional life in a nunnery (below).

these are what produced the "superior man," the gentleman. And that was the aim and goal of all the Confucian teaching—to produce the superior man.

"The princes [rulers] of today," he said, "are greedy in their search after material goods. . . . They take all they can from the people and invade the territory of good rulers against the will of the people, and they go out to get what they want without regard for what is right." Confucius arrays these five reciprocal attitudes, which really means ten, as the basic foundation of human relations: kindness in the father, filial piety in the son. Gentleness in the eldest brother, humility and respect in the younger. Right behavior in the husband, obedience in the wife. Consideration in the elders, deference in their juniors. Benevolence in rulers, loyalty in ministers, public servants and subjects. Where these obtain, order and harmony will reign.

In the psychology of an earlier day, there was a theory known as the James-Lange Theory, which said in effect that the emotion *follows* its manifestation, thus: Laugh and you will be cheerful. Weep and you will be sad. Some of the behavior prescribed by Confucius in the book of *Li* is reminiscent of that theory. For instance:

"When a father has just died, the son should appear quite overcome and as if he were at his wits' end. When the corpse has been laid in the coffin he should cast quick sorrowful glances this way and that, as if seeking for something which cannot be found. When the burial takes place he should look alarmed and restless, as if looking for one who does not return. At the end of the first year's mourning he should look sad and disappointed, and at the end of the second year he should have a vague and unreliant look."

There are many such prescriptions in the teachings of Confucius and, however bizarre they may seem to Occidentals, Chinese life was shaped by them for more than twenty centuries. One of his sayings was: "Wake yourself up with poetry, establish your character in *Li* and complete your education in music." As proof that he was in no way a religious mystic, this remark of his is sometimes adduced: "Respect the heavenly and earthly spirits and keep them at a distance." He also said that the superior man can find everything he needs within himself. A later and a greater Teacher declared that even the Kingdom of Heaven must be looked for within.

"I do not expect to find a saint today," said Confucius. "But if I find a gentleman I shall be quite satisfied." "A man who has a beautiful soul

Passing through convent courtyard in Chengtu processional, purple-robed Chinese nuns murmur prayers and sound instruments on way to temple. Their long vigils are broken only by pilgrimages and rare visitors.

always has some beautiful things to say, but a man who says beautiful things does not necessarily have a beautiful soul." "To know what you know and know what you don't know is the mark of one who knows." "If a man would be severe toward himself and generous toward others he would never arouse resentment."

The *Analects* abound in statements like those above. They were not all uttered in the bullet-shaped compactness in which we find them. The word *analects*, after all, means "gleanings." The sayings were gleaned not alone from his comments on the Classics, but from all his teaching career, from all the conversations with his disciples during years of communion and wandering about the land of China. Like all wise men, he was modest. To one of his disciples who paid him a compliment, he said, "If you were a rich man I would be your butler." The prayer of the Emperor Ching in the "Odes" might have been the prayer of Kung-Fu-tse, Confucius himself:

It is but as a little child I ask,
Without intelligence to do my task,
Yet learning, month by month, and
   day by day,

I will hold fast some gleams of knowledge bright.
Help me to bear my heavy burden right,
And show me how to walk in wisdom's way.

He loved the Odes. One day his son, Li, was passing hurriedly through the court and met his father standing alone, lost in thought.

"Have you read the Odes?"

"No," the young man answered. "Not yet."

"Then," said Confucius, "if you do not learn the Odes, you will not be fit to converse with."

If Confucius was not wholly happy in his son, he doubtless would have delighted in his grandson, Tsesze, to whom is attributed the book known as *The Doctrine of the Mean,* or *The Golden Mean.*

Dragons and stilts—traditional trappin
of all Chinese parades—also play part
religious processions. Thrashing drag
(left) drives evil spirits from Shangh
as textile workers help celebrate natior
holiday. "Confucius" on stilts (above) p
rades through Nanking streets duri
August 27 observance of birthday of t
Perfect Sage more than 2,500 years ag

In pilgrimage to Hangchow's Yao Fei Temple, Confucianists, Buddhists and Taoists (Chinese often belong to all three religions) rub stone faces of sages as means to grace and curative blessing. Prayer bead salesmen ply wares along routes leading to 12th century shrine and statue-studded courtyard. For 2,500 years, Confucian virtues of loyalty to oneself and charity to one's neighbor have molded the Chinese character.

For just as Plato went on writing dialogues illustrating the Socratic philosophy after the death of Socrates, so others, including this grandson Tsesze and the philosopher Mencius, went on expounding the teachings of Confucius. It has been said that Confucius was not strictly a religious man, and not a mystic. But in this book by his grandson, *The Golden Mean*, he comes nearest to being presented as both the one and the other. For example, when he is quoted as saying: "The moral law is a law from whose operation we cannot for one instant in our existence escape. A law from which we may escape is not the moral law—we seem to hear that other great Chinese teacher talking, Lao-Tse, who was the most mystical of Chinese, philosopher of the Tao, which is here rendered "the moral law." "The moral law is to be found everywhere and yet it is secret," Confucius is quoted as saying. "To find the central clue to our moral being which unites us to the universal order, that indeed is the highest human attainment." "Such," he said, "is the evidence of things invisible that it is impossible to doubt the spiritual nature of man." In that he joined all other great teachers.

Tradition has it that the two sages, the elder Lao-Tse, and the younger man, Kung Fu-tse, met at Loyang, the capital, where Lao-Tse was the keeper of the archives. Kung sought out all great men, all who could teach him anything. The old mystic is said to have given this piece of crusty advice to Confucius:

"I have heard that in times like these a good merchant, though he has rich treasures carefully stored away, appears as if he were poor, and that the superior man whose knowledge is complete, is yet to outward appearances stupid. Follow their example and put away your proud air and many vain desires, your insinuating habit of thought

**IMMENSE STONE FIGURES** of elephants decorate Ming tombs on outskirts of Nanking. Ming emperors, who ruled China from 1368 to 1644, revered Sage's memory by building temples in his honor and making birthday national holiday.

Faces of new and old China reflect harmony resulting from Confucian doctrine of *jen* or loving-kindness. Although historic culture centered in Confucianism is disrupted by communist rule, millions still revere Master and his rules of conduct. Confucius, as practical teacher, urged men to show "humanity" to each other.

and wild will which cannot prevail. These are of no advantage to you. That is all I have to tell you."

Confucius is quoted as declaring that "the wise man has no perplexities." But one cannot help feeling that remarks like Lao-Tse's above must have perplexed him considerably.

At the age of fifty, his biographers tell us, Confucius, who had lectured and theorized so much about government, finally achieved his dream of holding office. The Duke of Lu (his name was Ting) made him the magistrate of Chungtu. "After a year," we read, "the town became a model city for all its neighbors." By the time he was fifty-six, he was Minister of Justice and, according to some, Prime Minister. Biographers, of course, insist that forthwith honesty and morality improved to such an extent that things dropped in the street remained untouched until the owners came back and found them, and men and women walked on opposite sides of the street. But through intrigue and a cabal of the other ministers, who could not compete, Confucius was forced to resign and to leave the country.

For thirteen years he wandered about, attended by only three disciples, from one state to another, hoping that some prince or duke would appoint him to a ministry or an office. None did. His repu-

tation was great and some of the self-respecting rulers felt in duty bound to pay him homage and treat him courteously. But no one seemed to desire exposure to that monument of virtue. Some of the ministers, moreover, were so fearful of his greatness their own littleness drove them to a variety of tricks and devices to get rid of him. In some cases he was met by mobs, and in at least one instance he was actually imprisoned. Once, when he got detached from his friends who were searching for him, a peasant described him as looking like a stray dog. Confucius liked that description. He took a kind of pride in the fact that, for all his virtue and care for the welfare of China, he had not a place to lay his head.

In one state, that of Chu, where the ruler wanted to appoint Confucius to administer a district of about fifty square miles, a wily minister took the bull by the horns and admitted to the sovereign that no official in the land was the equal of Confucius. Indeed, so great were his abilities that a ruler took a grave risk in appointing him. He might soon overshadow everyone, including the monarch! The monarch decided not to appoint the sage. If ever a man was dis-appointed in the literal sense of the word, Confucius was that man.

Meanwhile, in his native state of Lu, things were

Tolerant Chinese, ranging from student at Peiping's Yenching University and director of Kunming's Wen Miao Temple (far left) to merchant in Hongkong and

scholar in Chengtu (above), find unifying philosophy in Confucius' *Five Classics*, his emphasis upon wisdom, and his maxim, "True goodness is loving your fellow men."

going from bad to worse. The ruler badly needed advice. Finally he sent for Confucius, and thus, after nearly fourteen years of exile, the sage returned to his native state. Did he get an appointment?

"It finally turned out," says a biographer, "that they could not make use of Master Kung in Lu. And neither did Master Kung strive for official position."

Age was creeping on. After his years of wandering, he felt tired. Always forthright and truthful, he was now perhaps a shade overcandid. When Baron Kang, one of the rulers of his province, asked Confucius how to lessen the petty thieving going on in the land, he received a very straight answer:

"Sir, if you were not so avaricious and did not countenance thefts yourself, the people would not steal, even though you rewarded them for it." Few rulers would like to receive answers like that. If reform was to begin at the top instead of the bottom, why, what was the world coming to? Rulers don't want reformers of that stripe. And Confucius was too wise not to know it. He expected to pass into obscurity and oblivion directly after his death. His modesty equaled his greatness. He could not imagine that his would become the most famous name in China.

During his last years, saddened by disappointment, he occupied himself with study and writing. He edited the Classics, he wrote *Spring and Autumn*, a chronicle or history of the preceding two and a half centuries, and slowly prepared for the final event. He saw a portent when in a hunt by the gentry of his native land, a *chin lin*, or unicorn, was killed. A similar animal was connected with the Sage's birth legends. He was greatly depressed by it. Two of his favorite disciples passed away, causing him heavy grief. He felt ill. Tse Kung, the last of the favorites, hurried to his side. "Why are you so late in coming?" demanded Confucius. And to himself he murmured, "The mountain is crumbling, the pillar is toppling, the old philosopher is fading away." He died a few days later.

Even after the Sun Yat-sen revolution, the temples of Confucius in all China remained intact. The one in the Forbidden City at Peiping, for example, is still as plain and peaceful as a Unitarian meetinghouse in New England, adorned only with the commemorative tablets of Kung Futse and his disciples. Those temples and the creed they represent supplied the dominant strain in Chinese ethical and religious life. Whether they will continue to do so, now and henceforth, remains to be seen.

Spacious splendor of Peiping's walled and moated Forbidden City was executed by China's Ming and Manchu
emperors over period of 500 years. Throne Hall of
Supreme Harmony, standing 110 feet high and surrounded by terraced courtyards and marble stairways,
is most impressive religious shrine in China. In this
great Confucian ceremonial hall, China's emperors
once sat. In Hall of Middle Harmony and Hall of Pro-

tecting Harmony (rear), they received visiting princes. In careful arrangement of buildings and courtyards, Chinese demonstrate that love of order and virtuous balance which their "Uncrowned King" exemplified.

Today, with all China wracked by God-denying Communism, the silent people may yet heed their beloved Master Kung, "Following virtue is like ascending a mountain; following vice is like rushing down a precipice."

# 4. TAOISM

*The Heavenly Way which draws all men together in unity of heart and soul*

THE PICTURE CALLED UP IN OUR minds by the name of Lao-Tse is that of an old, a very old, Chinese philosopher, with a flowing white beard, driving a plodding bullock cart away from the populous capital of ancient China toward less congested regions. He was turning his back on the chicanery, insincerity and intrigue of the city. After a lifetime of service as librarian of the royal archives, the old man was now going west into the mountains to die, and going alone. The picture is faintly ridiculous and infinitely touching.

At the northwestern gate of the city, the keeper of the gate, Yin Hsi, saluted the old man and said:

"Sir, you are about to withdraw yourself and far out of sight. I pray you first to compose a book for me."

Which was quite a request. Not merely an autograph, but a book. Lao-Tse, however, was vastly obliging. The Chinese historian, Szuma Ch'ien, tells us: "On this request Lao-Tse wrote a book in two parts, setting forth his views on the Way and Virtue in five thousand characters."

What happened then? It is related that the philosophical gatekeeper thereupon got into the cart with Lao-Tse, and the bullock, without breaking any speed limits, we may be sure, moved away into the middle distance. We never hear again of Yin Hsi, the gatekeeper, nor was Lao-Tse himself ever seen again. How did the book survive to gain currency and come down through the ages? We are not told. That book is the "Book of the Tao."

Its five thousand words, more or less, have since become one of the world's great classics, and its content one of the great religious philosophies. There are dozens of translations and scores of commentaries on the book. Yet new translations and interpretations keep appearing. Its full title is *Tao Teh King*, which might be rendered The Way Of Virtue Canon. Lao-Tse left no other writing about himself or his philosophy than this little book.

Young Taoist monks leave Wewan temple after devotions led by lord abbot (center). Remainder of day will be spent in reading and study without severity of discipline found in many Eastern and Western religious orders. Although Chinese people often belong simultaneously to Taoist, Buddhist and Confucian faiths, Taoism generally is religion of common people. Shorn of its 2,000-year accretions of idolatry and witchcraft, Taoism teaches doctrine of Inner Kingdom and through its unfoldment development of peace, love, humility and harmony. "It is the Way of Heaven not to strive," said Lao-Tse, "and yet it knows how to overcome."

Annual pilgrimage to Temples at Kunming finds hundreds of men and women resting at picnic grounds before walking to hillside shrine inscribed, "In the vessel of heaven lies another world." Taoists believe that behind lesser deities such as Kitchen God and Earth God stands Great *Tao* or Heavenly Way which is everywhere.

Tiny Taoist shrine along road gets offerings of rice and money from pilgrims who seek inner purification and exorcising of outside demons. Peasant woman (below), praying way through "Ten Courts of Purgatory," completes rites of pilgrimage. Good Taoists also pray to trinity of metaphysical powers called "Three Pure Ones."

So little is known about him, some doubt his very existence. That, however, is not unusual with a great man. The historian in a brief sketch informs us that Lao-Tse was born in 604 B.C.—though scholars have since moved that date to 570 B.C.—in the state of Chu, now part of Honan Province. Also, that he was the keeper of the archives in the royal library at Loyang, and that he departed in the manner we have seen. That is all.

The book of his teaching is almost as brief as his biography. Yet Lin Yutang declares that if there is any book that can claim to interpret for us the spirit of the Orient, or the essential character of Chinese behavior, it is the Book of the Tao. Not only is the book profound, it is written in a gnomic, compressed style, giving to almost every sentence the impact of a bullet. Lao-Tse speaks of earlier philosophers as "sentence makers." He himself was not only a sentence maker, but a paradox maker. He loved to utter things like this:

Burning incense sticks as talisman before tablet of religion's mystical founder, Chinese woman (above) pauses in prayer before proceeding on to main temple. Monk (below), meditating on temple stool, exemplifies essence of Taoism—radical piety and a Quaker-like quietism which Lao-Tse called "life of Inner Kingdom."

Within temple, Chinese soldiers study statued "helpers" of Lao-Tse who urged his followers to "accumulate virtue and store up merit; treat all with gentleness and love, be loyal, be dutiful, be respectful; be upright yourselves in order that you may reform others; do not injure even little insects or grass or trees."

"The most genuine cleverness appears as stupidity." "A victory should be celebrated as a funeral." "He who knows does not speak; he who speaks does not know."

The word *Tao* means the Way, the Way of Heaven, the Way of Nature, the Way of Taoist living. But as the name of the philosophy and religion of the Tao, it has come to mean the universal cosmic energy behind all creation, omnipresent, impersonal and eternal. Its action is silent, almost unnoticed. "All things spring up without a word spoken," said Lao-Tse, and one hears nothing of claims or assertions. If the government of men could proceed in that sure, silent way, this would be a beautiful world. The nearest to a definition Lao-Tse gives is: "The Tao that can be known is not the absolute Tao. The names you can give it are not the ultimate names."

"Conceived of as having no name, it is the Originator of heaven and earth. Conceived of as having a name, it is the Mother of creation."

When old Taoists feel death approaching, they often retire to such hotels as Singapore's "Death House" to pass last days in meditation and prayer. Looking upon "Death as going home," they know "Tao is sanctuary where all things find refuge, the good man's priceless treasure, the savior of him who is not good."

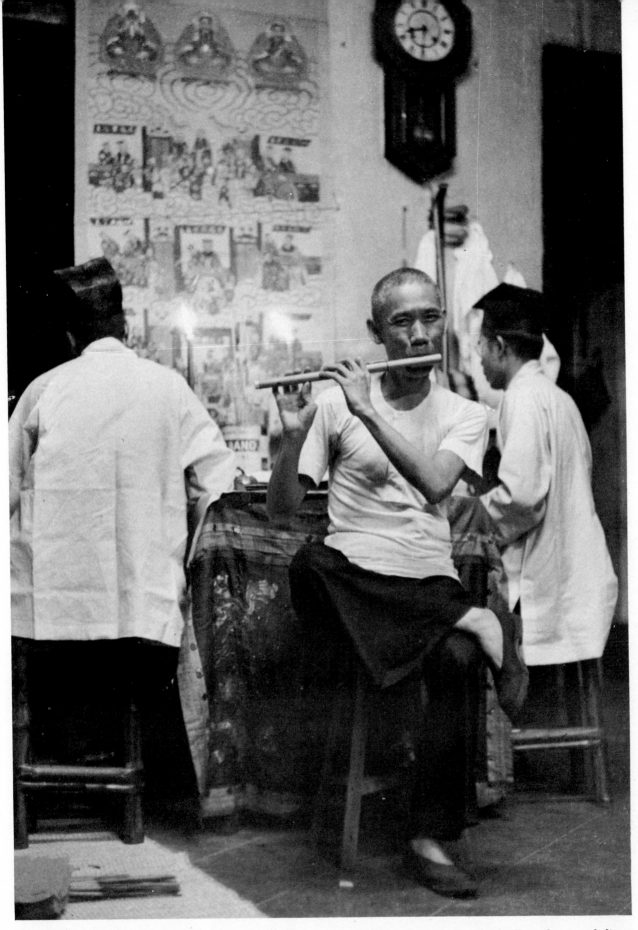

Cheerful priest plays musical tribute in "Death House," as funeral proceeds downstairs. Several hundred persons occupy hotel, and it is felt most important there be proper reverence for death. For, devotees believe with their master mystic, Lao-Tse, "He who knows that life and death are one is he who cultivates life best."

This reminds one of "That" of the Upanishads or the *Ka* of the Rig-Veda, "whose true being remains unknown and unknowable." Tao, briefly, is That in which all things have their origin. It is the very essence of all things. This is a far more mystical concept than anything to be found in Confucius. We know of the purgation and purifications required of novices in all mystical schools in any religion and in all Eastern yogas. Lao-Tse prescribes similar requisites.

"Only the man eternally free from passion," he declares, "can contemplate its [the Tao's] spiritual essence. He who is clogged by desires can know no more than its outer form. These two things, the spiritual and the material, though we call them by different names, are one and the same in their origin. This sameness is a mystery, the mystery of mysteries. It is the gate of all that is subtle and wonderful."

Buddha, it may be recalled, prescribed the Eightfold Path as a means of putting an end to suffering by eliminating desire. Lao-Tse in far-off China, made desirelessness a condition for reaching the Tao:

> Always without desire we must be found,
> If its deep mystery we would sound;
> But he who by desire is bound
> Sees the mere shell of things around.

Our own Christian Scripture tells us that only the pure in heart shall see God, and non-attachment in one form or another is insisted upon by all religions. Lao-Tse, however, stresses not so much the piety of our demeanor as its wisdom. To him, the latter embraces the former. Some, indeed many, of the eighty-one chapters in the book are too compressed for general comprehension. Hence the numerous translations and commentaries. If we try to read, say, chapter XVI, it seems to us bafflingly obscure. "The state of vacancy," we are told, "should be brought to the utmost degree, and that of stillness guarded with unwearying vigor." That translation is a literal English one. But a Chinese scholar, who happens to be a Buddhist monk, Brother Wai-Tao, renders the paragraphs from his own mystical point of view like this:

"At the moment when one is able to concentrate his mind to the extreme of emptiness and is able to hold it there in serene tranquillity, then his spirit is unified with the spirit of the universe and it has returned to its original state from which his mind and all things in the universe have emerged as appearance."

Perhaps this rendering is a little too subtle for most minds. We return to the English scholar, James Legge, in the *Sacred Books of the East* series:

"When things in the vegetable world have displayed their luxuriant growth, we see each of them

Temple at Eastern Hills, a center of Taoism for 1,500 years, recently was closed by Communists. Today, as China's crisis mounts, Lao-Tse's advice is more pertinent than ever: be pure and humble; heed little outward rituals, but develop your inner consciousness in harmony with Tao; then everything else will take care of itself.

return to its root. This returning to the root is what we call the state of stillness; and the stillness may be called a reporting that they have fulfilled their appointed end.

"The report of that fulfilment is the regular, unchanging rule. To know that unchanging rule is to be intelligent; not to know it leads to wild movements and evil issues. The knowledge of that unchanging rule produces a grand capacity and forbearance, and that capacity and forbearance lead to a community of feeling with all things. From this community of feeling comes a kingliness of character; and he who is king-like goes on to be Heaven-like. In that likeness to Heaven he possesses the Tao. Possessed of the Tao, he endures long; and to the end of his bodily life, is exempt from all danger of decay."

According to this order, life begins not at forty or at four, but with the acquisition of that king-like, heaven-like character that brings tolerance, forbearance and community of feeling with all things,

which is the realization of oneness. That is possessing Tao. How does he know all this? By virtue of the Tao.

> The grandest forms of active force
> From Tao come, their only source.
> Who can of Tao the nature tell?
> Our sight it flies, our touch as well.

Yet subtle and elusive though it is, it is the source and origin of all things. To this primal essence, the One, Lao-Tse in common with all other Teachers, returns again and again. For our ego-centered natures it is no easy concept to grasp. Yet to grasp it is the goal of all striving. It must be hammered into our consciousness. "How self-sufficing it is," he exclaims, "and how changeless! How omnipresent and infinite! Yet this tranquil emptiness becomes the Mother of all. Who knows its name? I can only characterize it and call it Tao. Though it is quite inadequate, I will even call it the Great." We note

Priests in elegantly embroidered robes emerge from Peiping's Temple of Eastern Hills. Besides worshiping Heavenly Tao which "overspreads and sustains all things," priests serve people as doctors, astrologists, exorcisers of devils.

Mother God (above) in Tung-Yueh-Miao Temple in Peiping is favorite shrine of city's expectant mothers. Religious relic shop (below) in Canton displays dresses and "money" pyramids for souls of the dead.

how he apologizes for calling it great, since any qualification is a limitation. We say God is. Lao-Tse said the same thing of the Tao. "Was he groping after God," speculates Dr. Legge, "if haply he might find Him?" Today he would scarcely ask this question. The concept of God has broadened.

Like all the great Teachers, Lao-Tse was untroubled by doubts, speculations or vacillations. He knew his mind because he stuck to his Tao. He was a servant of royalty in the imperial capital. Yet he declared boldly:

"If anyone desires to take and remake the empire under his own reforming plans, he will never be successful. The empire is a spiritual thing that cannot be remade after one's own ideas, and he who attempts it will only a make a failure. Even he who tries to hold it will lose it."

In his terse, epigrammatic manner he hammered on the ideas that were to him paramount. The all-inclusiveness and perfection of the Tao, the supreme unity of all things merging into the One, simplicity, quietude and calmness, the shunning of violence and force, *wu-wei,* inaction—by which he meant non-interference, true humility and spirituality—these were the principles that made for life. Their contraries led to failure and destruction.

"The Tao is ever inactive and yet there is nothing that it does not do."

"When a minister serves a ruler after the principle of Tao," wrote Lao-Tse, "he will not advise a resort to force of arms to become a great nation. Like returns to like. So briars and thorns grow rank where an army camps. Bad years of want and disorder follow a great war."

"Both arms and armor," he said, "are unblessed things. Not only do men come to detest them, but a curse seems to follow them. Therefore the one who follows the principle of the Tao does not resort to arms."

"I am teaching," he adds later, "the same thing which is taught by others; others have said the strong and aggressive do not come to natural deaths, but I make this saying the basis of my teaching."

Every great teacher teaches humility, yet almost nobody has learned it. Failure to learn it is devastating, yet people pride themselves on ignoring it.

"He who knows other men is discerning; he who knows himself is intelligent. He who overcomes others is strong; he who overcomes himself is mighty. He who is satisfied with his lot is rich.

"Grasping and hoarding invite waste and loss both of property and life. A contented person is never dishonored. One who knows how to stop with enough is free from danger; he will endure."

Carrying bird cage and flanked by followers, Taoist priest takes part in Shanghai parade. 20th-century Taoism numbers 50 million adherents and complements Confucianism's practical ethics with supernatural theology. →

Ancient and modern pagodas maintain China's picturesque architecture. 13-story temple (above), located outside Peiping, was built in 472 A.D., while Hong Kong's glittering White Pagoda (left) is barely 20 years old.

Chinese love of spectacle reaches religious extremes in demon-frightening giants heading funeral in Peiping and in brilliantly lighted tea-houses marking Moon Festival in Hong Kong (below). Taoism, injecting color and romance into life and art, fostered appreciation of beauty where Confucianism emphasized goodness.

All these things and many more, he tells us, he knows because of Tao, whose "way is wide and straight for men to follow, but most people prefer the bypaths."

That is the most costly of aberrations, wandering away from the broad highway of the Tao. For: "When the potentiality of Tao manifests itself, it becomes the Mother of all things. When one realizes that his life comes from this universal Mother, he will also realize his brotherhood to all her descendants. When one realizes his descent from the universal Mother and his brotherhood with all humanity, he will cherish his life and thus, to its end, will be kept in perfect health."

Lao-Tse in China in the sixth century B.C. taught how the Tao becomes the Mother of all things. Jesus at the other end of Asia in the first century A.D. was forever about His Father's business and doing His Father's will. Ramakrishna, the nineteenth-century saint whom his devotees call an avatar, a divine incarnation, was dedicated to the worship of his Divine Mother.

The governing of states occupied Lao-Tse to perhaps a lesser degree than Confucius, but both those Chinese sages devoted much of their thought to government.

"In governing people," held Lao-Tse, "and in worshipping heaven nothing surpasses the Teh or virtue of self-restraint. The restraint of desire is like returning to the original Tao. Returning to one's origin means the recovery of one's vitality. When one has recovered his original vitality, nothing is unmanageable. If nothing is unmanageable, then he retains his original tranquillity, because he is unconscious of any limits. When he retains this state of tranquillity he may govern the country wisely. Moreover, when he is in a state of tranquillity he will govern the country as a mother takes care of her children and by so doing long retain his usefulness. He will be like a plant having a strong stem and deep roots. He will manifest the longevity of the Tao."

"Governing a great state is like cooking small fish," is a famous aphorism of Lao-Tse. That is, government must not be overdone. Non-interference, or what we call *laissez-faire*, and humility are the favorite themes of Lao-Tse.

"The female always overcomes the male by her quietude. Quietude may be considered a sort of abasement."

"He who lightly promises is sure to keep but little faith."

"The tree which fills the arms grew from the

tiniest sprout. The journey of a thousand li commenced with a single step."

"The sage wishing to be above men, puts himself by his words below them, and wishing to be before them, places his person behind them."

"The wise man is he alone who rests satisfied with what he has."

"I have three precious things which I prize and hold fast. The first is gentleness, the second is economy; and the third is shrinking from taking precedence of others."

"The wise man does not accumulate; the more he gives to others the more he has for himself."

"Recompense injury with kindness," he taught. "To those who are good, I am good, and to those who are not good, I am also good; thus all get to be good. To those who are sincere, I am sincere, and to those who are not sincere, I am also sincere; and thus all get to be sincere."

Such were some of the sayings of Lao-Tse in his wisdom-packed little book, the *Tao Teh King*. Almost every line of it is quotable and that is one of the marks of greatness. There are those who say there is no religion in the book; then, how could it give birth to a religion? Certainly, if by religion is meant worship of diverse gods, rituals and ceremonies, the Tao Teh King is barren of them. But if by religion is meant faith in a Supreme One, one without a second, what Vedanta expresses as Existence Absolute, Knowledge Absolute, Bliss Absolute, *Satchidananda* in the Sanskrit word, then Lao-Tse made available to the Chinese world something to which only vague references had existed before him. The Absolute Brahman has held India together until the present day. Possibly the Tao may save China. The human spirit can unite with Tao. But how can it unite with dialectic materialism?

It must not be supposed, however, that as soon as the little book was written it gained immediate currency and its philosophy became a religion. First it needed some great disciple, who was also a popularizer, to spread its teaching abroad. We know what Plato in his dialogues did for the ideas of Socrates. The Chinese philosopher Mencius did as much for Confucius. And so, similarly, Chuang-tse, who lived about two hundred years after Lao-Tse, embraced the philosophy of the Tao and spent his life and his genius expounding it, with great force and delightful humor.

The strong mystical element in the Tao Teh King soon caused many a mystic and contemplative to try living according to its teachings, to practice breathing and to seek means for longevity. Confu-

Ninghsia City, in China's Moslem northwest, boasts a Taoist temple and school for province's 20,000 followers of Lao-Tse. Temple attendant (above) beats fish-head drum summoning faithful to worship at altar adorned with image of Prophet and inevitable flying dragon. Children (below) enjoy recess in school park.

cianism has been said to be a religion for gentlemen. The common people could not always understand the fine-drawn points of conduct. But with Taoism it was different. Those men who withdrew to caves, to forest huts, or even to hollow trees, to practice Taoism, seemed to the people to be not only saints, but even magicians. Some actually pretended to be magicians and to possess the secrets of longevity, of the elixir of life, how to exorcise undesirable demons, how to improve one's fortunes.

As an organized religion, that is, as a church, Taoism came into being only in the first century A.D., some six hundred years after Lao-Tse. One Chang Tao-Ling, said to have possessed great magical powers, founded a kind of dynasty, and his heirs actually created a state in Szechwan, based on the Taoist teaching. The influence of Buddhism during the first six centuries of our era hastened the development of Taoism into a system with monastic orders, priests, monasteries, temples and a pantheon of gods of which the modest Lao-Tse was made the chief! In 1016 the government presented the Taoist hierarchy a fief, a sort of papal state, in Kiangsi Province, and for all we know the T'ien-shi, as he calls himself, the "Heaven Master," reigns there today as the chief of the Taoist hierarchy. Present-day Taoism with its elixirs, longevity pills, animism and magic is far from the lofty philosophy of the Tao Teh King. Other religions, too, have degenerated from their high birth and station. From time to time a reform sets in and they are again raised toward their original pure state. Perhaps some day that will happen to Taoism.

As late as the fourteenth century, a Chinese emperor, the founder of the Ming dynasty, while browsing in his library, came across the Tao Teh King. He was impressed by this statement of Lao-Tse: "If the people do not fear death, how then can you frighten them by death?" The people, observes the Emperor, were at that time obstinate and the magistrates corrupt.

"Almost every morning," he goes on, "ten men were executed in public: by the same evening a hundred had committed the same crimes. Did not this justify the thought of Lao-Tse? From that time I ceased to inflict capital punishment. I imprisoned the guilty and imposed fines. In less than a year my heart was comforted. I recognized then that in this book is the perfect source of all things. It is the sublime Master of Kings and the inestimable treasure of the people."

Perhaps someone like that Ming emperor will again rule China.

Standing amid storied columns and gilded statues of beloved Chinese saints, Taoist and Buddhist priests pray for world peace in Hangchow's beautiful Ling Ying Temple. Recognizing identity of the Everlasting Tao and Eternal Nirvana, both leaders and followers of

the two great faiths easily worship and work together. Taoists, striving to walk in the Way of Heaven, seek ultimate perfection of Tao with its repose, tranquillity, stillness and inaction. They cultivate the Inner Kingdom and by "the practice of Inner Life stillness con-

tinually conquer all things." And, like their spiritual brothers in every world religion, they go about doing good. For, as their Old Philosopher told Chinese people 2,500 years ago, "Hold fast to gentleness, frugality, humility. We must be at peace in order to be active in love."

# 5. SHINTO

## *Sincerity is the single virtue binding God and man in one*

AMONG THE RELIGIONS MAN IS following today, Shinto, the national religion practiced by 70,000,000 Japanese, appears rudimentary. The nearest to a Supreme Deity in its content is the Sun Goddess, *Amaterasu Omikami,* from whom the sacred Japanese emperors are descended in an unbroken line, it is asserted, to this day.

But how did the ancestral Sun Goddess attain to her place and position? It came about in this way. When chaos had separated into Heaven and earth there dwelt on the Plain of High Heaven innumerable deities much as men live on earth. Two of the deities, Izanagi, the male-who-invites, and Izanami, the female-who-invites, were elected by their fellow divinities to create, consolidate and give birth to the Islands of Japan. So the two divinities descended by the Floating Bridge of Heaven (Rainbow), and when they reached the lower end of this bridge, they began to create—in this wise. Izanagi pushed down his jeweled spear into the muddy, briny mess and churned it until it became thick and glutinous. When he withdrew the spear "the brine which dripped from the point of the spear coagulated and formed an island." That was Onagoro-Jima, the Self-Coagulating Island.

According to *Nihongi,* a scripture

Mt. Fujiyama, Japan's sacred mountain and dominating symbol of national life, rises 12,388 feet above Numazu City. Bell-ringing pilgrims, who climb peak, chant, "May our six senses be pure."

dated A.D. 720, Izanagi and Izanami became husband and wife, settled on that island and set about producing a family of lands and countries. The first fruits of their conjugal union were the eight major islands of Japan. After that they produced a number of deities, some thirty-five in all, the last offspring being Kagu-Tsuchi, the God of Fire. In giving birth to this fiery god, Izanami was so badly burned that she sickened and died.

When after her death Izanami departed for the dark land of Yomi, the disconsolate Izanagi followed her, hoping to induce her to return with him to the world above. But he was even less fortunate than Orpheus and Euridice. For, when he found her, Izanami upbraided him: "My lord and husband, why is thy coming so late? . . . Do not look on me." But he did look and what he saw horrified him. Her body had already begun to decompose and maggots were swarming over it. Shocked, he exclaimed, "What a hideous and polluted land I have come to"—and he fled.

That visit to the nether regions had important consequences.

"Why didst thou not observe that which I charged thee?" cried after him the indignant Izanami. "Now am I put to shame!" And she sent the Ugly Females of Yomi to pursue her husband and to slay him. He managed to elude them by

Symbol of Shinto to 70 million Japanese, a huge *Torii* rises from sea on Shrine Island of Miyajima. Today, with State Shinto abolished, believers belong to 13 sects, cherish ancient truth, "Whatever is, is divine spirit."

pelting them with peaches. But at the Even Pass of Yomi, the gateway, Izanami herself caught up with him. He seized a great rock, blocked the way and utered the words, "Our relationship is severed." That was the formula for divorce.

The very first thing he wanted upon his return from Yomi was a bath to get rid of the pollution inevitable in that sad country. He leaped into the sea. His washing of himself gave birth to a number of deities including the God of Good and Bad Luck. When he washed out his left eye, the dirt of that became the Sun Goddess. The dirt from his right eye became the Moon God, and Susa-no-wo, the Storm God, came from his nostrils. Many a scholar has wondered how a people, so noted for love of beauty, came to have a mythology like this.

Who and what are the Japanese? For all their present homogeneity, they are a mixed people— part Mongolian, part Korean, part South Pacific Islanders. The islands of Japan, however Izanagi and Izanami created them, were inhabited by an aboriginal people, the Ainu, sometimes called the hairy Ainus. They are short, with long wavy hair, and the men are generally bearded. They are about as rare a sight now as one of our American Indians. But anyone who has seen them is certain they are Caucasians, some truncated offshoot of the white race. The Japanese at some early date displaced them and drove them to the northern islands.

Evidently the Ainu were stubborn fighters, for it took the invaders a long time to drive them out of coveted sites. Bows, arrows, weapons became so important they received the reverence and worship accorded to the *Kami*, or gods. Great warriors were, likewise, given exaggerated honors. Ancestor worship and nature worship created gods by the thousand. There were said to be "800 myriads" of them. Every clan had its chieftains, its military heroes and its gods—all were Kami. Kami, Kami, everywhere, as the shrines that dot the landscape and the roadsides of Japan attest to this hour.

It was Izanagi, we recall, who gave birth to the Sun Goddess, and also to her brother, Susa-no-wo, the turbulent Storm God. He was a rude, noisy deity, who was assigned to be ruler of the nether region. Before going there to take up office, he ascended to Heaven to say farewell to his sister, the Sun Goddess. She did not like his manners and, before going forth to meet him, took the precaution of arraying herself not only in a jeweled necklace, but in manly garb which included a sword and bow and arrows. They stood facing each other on opposite sides of the River of Heaven, as the Chinese call the Milky Way.

**HIGH PRIESTS MARCH** from Holy of Holies at Isé, after

ceremony honoring Emperor Meiji, who made Shinto state religion in 1868. 100,000 such shrines now dot Nippon.

*Meiji-Tanno-Sai* is summer festival commemorating death of Emperor Meiji in 1912. Gaily garbed ceremonial dancers and flute-playing Komuso priests (above) take part in three-day celebration which fea- tures "Play Day," "Flower Day" and "Holy-of-Holies Day." In historic Kasuga Shrine (below), located in Nara Park and originally built in 768, virgins dressed in traditional red and white execute ritual Kagura dance.

Picturesque Shinto festivals mark every season and national holiday, as New Year's fete (above and below) in Tokyo. *Gengaku* musicians and *Bugaku* dancers, who belong to Imperial household, give public performance to help priests and people celebrate New Year when all Japanese become year older. Prayers are offered, homes decorated with pine and bamboo symbolizing courage and constancy, and nobody goes to bed until dawn.

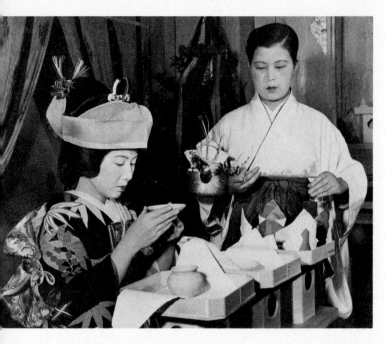

Shinto marriages, which take place in groom's home, are family affair in which bride (above) dons colorful kimono and newlyweds sip saké from red lacquer bowls. *Geishas* or glamour girls (below) often prettify wedding parties as well as rice and flower festivals.

His intentions, Susa-no-wo called across to his sister, were strictly honorable. He suggested that they produce some children, but by a singular method. This method, somewhat reminiscent of our facts-of-life explanations of the birds and the bees, was to bite off parts of the jewels and swords they were each wearing, crunch them thoroughly and blow away the fragments into space. That seemed a harmless plan enough, and eight children came into being this way. Various Japanese families claim descent from those children, but the important thing is that one of the families is that of the Mikados. That is how the Mikados came to be descended from the Sun Goddess.

Susa-no-wo has already been described as rude, but he was even worse than that. He was unseemly and shocking. He let loose the piebald colt of Heaven in his sister's rice fields and sacred weaving hall, and even committed unmentionable nuisances in her hall while she was having a celebration. In her chagrin and indignation the Sun Goddess withdrew herself into the Rock-cave of Heaven, leaving the world to unmitigated darkness.

The consternation among the heavenly deities was great. They tried various devices by which to lure the Sun Goddess from her cave. One of them was to dig up a Sakaki tree of Heaven with five hundred branches. On the high branches they hung strings of jewels, on the middle branches a mirror and on the lower branches pieces of cloth. They recited a liturgy in her honor. It availed them nothing. Then Ame no Uzume, "the Dread Female of Heaven," mounted a tub and danced an indecent dance, which made all the eight hundred myriads of gods shake the very Plain of Heaven with their laughter. The goddess in the cave, wondering how they could laugh with so much abandon when she had left the world in darkness, opened the door a crack. Strong hands seized her at once and she was prevented from re-entering the cave. They presented her with the mirror and the necklace of jewels—two of the sacred treasures every Japanese emperor receives at his coronation. The third, the sword, was later found in the tail of a dragon by Susa-no-wo.

The story of the Sun Goddess and the Rock-cave is the central myth of the Shinto religion, and is also the origin of some of the most important ceremonies. Many other events, symbolic of later beliefs and practices, occurred after the emergence of the Sun Goddess. But the most important was this. Amaterasu Omikami was looking down upon the islands of Japan and, turning to her grandson, Ninigi, she informed him that her descendants were

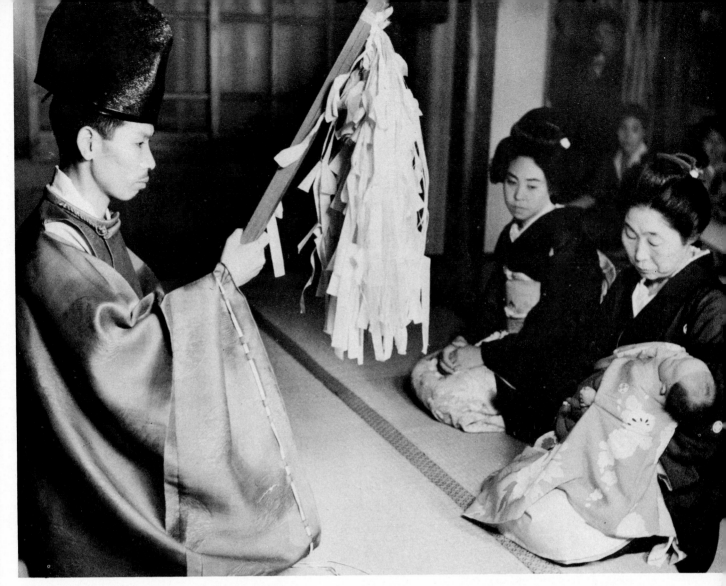

Carried by grandmother and watched by mother, infant is baptized in Nagasaki shrine. Priest purifies baby by waving *gohei* or paper mace and giving him a name carefully chosen for good luck. Shinto, which Lafcadio Hearn called the religion of loyalty, stresses family ties, ancestor worship, devotion to fatherland, Emperor and "heavenly Kami." Like the Chinese, Japanese revere Confucius as master teacher of the art of living.

the ordained rulers of that island realm. "Do thou, my August Grandchild, proceed thither and govern it. Go, and may prosperity attend thy dynasty, and may it, like Heaven and Earth, endure forever."

So saying, she gave him the three treasures, the necklace, the mirror and the sword, and told him to look upon the mirror as though it were herself. Ninigi, obedient to his grandmother, "thrusting apart the eight-piled clouds of Heaven, clove his way with an awful way-cleaving and descended to earth." He first touched on the island of Kyushu, married and begot children. The grandschild of one of them was Jimmu Tenno, the first human sovereign of Japan who supposedly began his reign at Yamato in 660 B.C.

That many-sided American astronomer and philosopher, Percival Lowell, who wrote upon esoteric and occult Japan, interpreted the Japanese mythology as a prolonged childish and adolescent paternal fear. "The Japanese," he said, "have stayed boys. To the Japanese eye the universe took on the paternal look. Parental awe, which these people understood, lent explanation to natural dread, which they did not. Quite simply, to their minds the thunder and the wind, the sunshine and the shower, were the work not only of anthropomorphic beings, but of beings ancestrally related to themselves. In short, Shinto, their explanation of things in general, is nothing else than the patriarchal principle projected without perspective into the past, dilating with distance into deity."

W. G. Aston, however, a profound student of the Japanese language, literature and religion and translator of the *Nihongi* scripture, takes the more tol-

Shinto, around which art and beauty of Japanese life still largely revolve, emphasizes worship of a myriad nature gods. Elaborate idol (above), vividly imaging God of Hunting at a Nikko shrine, typifies one of the thousands of spirits honored by Shinto votaries.

erant view that students of religion generally nowadays take of polytheism. The inanimate universe is not really inanimate, but "instinct with sentient life." The innumerable deities are in reality a way of expressing this sense of all-pervading life. While polytheism is not a high form of religion, it is as high as its devotees can grasp. "The emotional basis of religion," he believes, "is gratitude, love, and hope, rather than fear. . . . Shinto is essentially a religion of gratitude and love." He points out that the Sun Goddess and the Food Deity are beneficent beings. When the Sun Goddess emerged from the cave, the text records: "Heaven at length became clear, and all people could see each other's faces distinctly. They stretched forth their hands and

danced and sang together, exclaiming 'Oh! how delightful! how pleasant! how clear!' "

The story that the Mikados are descended from the Sun Goddess is simply a way of honoring the sovereign, the Japanese equivalent of the divine right of kings. Without these and similar vital elements, declares Mr. Aston, "Japanese myth would be nothing more than what some writers have supposed it, a farrago of absurdities, and its examination would belong not to the physiology, but to the pathology of the human mind."

Nevertheless, Shinto (the word is of Chinese origin) was and is the national religion of some seventy million Japanese, and for some fifteen centuries of Nipponese history it has been known as the Way of the Gods. It is a polytheism, possessing no Supreme Deity, no moral code, and is practically without recognition of a future state. There is a general absence of a deep earnest faith, and its conception of spirit is of the feeblest. As to its gods, who can classify them when, according to Shinto, they number as high as 800 or even 1,500 myriads? They include every conceivable kind of nature god, spirits, heavenly bodies, even qualities—all are worshiped almost indiscriminately. There are earth gods, mountain gods, sea gods, river gods, well gods, wind gods, fire gods, house gods, tree gods, gate gods, even privy gods. In the seventh century ranks were introduced into Japan from China. Not only men, but gods, too, were given ranks, and many a god

**Yomei-Mon Gate at Nikko, one of Japan's most**

ranked lower than the higher grade government officials. At times, gods even received promotions.

The pantheon of Shinto abounds in specialists, like a modern army. For instance Nomi no Sukune, a god of wrestling, was doubtless a great wrestler in his lifetime. And the writer, Lafcadio Hearn, tells of a farmer who was deified because he deserved well of his neighbors. He saved them from a tidal wave by setting on fire his own rice crop in order to draw them away from the seashore. They declared the man a god, built a temple dedicated to his spirit, and there in the shrine they worshiped as a divinity him who was still living on the hill above in an old thatched hut. Many other men have been so deified—doctors, soothsayers, flower arrangers, carpenters, blacksmiths, merchants. Needless to say, all Mikados are Kami.

Worship in the Shinto creed is not elaborate. Anyone who has visited shrines in Japan is struck by two phenomena—the absence of rites and the presence of reverence. Bowing to the shrine of the god is the general way of showing it. Two bows before the prayer or offering and two after is the custom. Offerings of food and drink, rice and *saké*, are the usual things. The offerings to the Sun Goddess and the Food Goddess at the Shrine in Isé consist of four cups of sake, sixteen saucers of rice, and four of salt, "besides, fish, birds, fruit, seaweed, and vegetables." The *Mitama,* or spirit of the god, inhabits his temple and appreciates the offerings.

plendent temples, stands 25 feet high and 22 feet long.

Japanese high school girls greet salutation of the sunrise, after reaching peak of 12,388-foot Mt. Fuji. 50,000 white-robed pilgrims climb snow-capped mountain each summer, stop at ten teahouses dotting steep trails, finally pray at summit shrine of Fuji goddess.

The very name Shinto came into currency only in the sixth century A.D., when the coming of Buddhism to Japan created nothing short of a revolution. A complete transformation in the life of the Japanese took place under the Chinese and Buddhist influences. Not until the nineteenth century, under the impact of Western civilization, did Japan experience so epochal a change. The loose, haphazard nature worship now took on a markedly Confucian cast, both in morals and in filial piety. Ancestor worship now took on the dimensions of a cult. The Emperor's descent from the Sun Goddess was emphasized, and other families began to assert their descent from deities as close as possible to the Sun Goddess. Even the common people were declared to be divinely descended, though, of course, from lesser and more distant deities. If Shinto was the Way of the Gods, all Japanese were the offspring of the gods. This was the germ of the master-race

Boy's confirmation, which is important rite on road to manhood, often takes place outdoors to chant of priestly prayers and cleansing ablutions. Shinto, stressing inner and outer purity, avows, "Actions sincere, by noble-minded man, reflect very Self of the Unseen."

Boys' Festival, which is quaint fête celebrating growth of country's millions of sons, gives youths chance to strut their stuff in Kyushu. Dancer drummers, beating tomtoms, move in rhythmic circles. Youth training also includes courtesy, self-control and reverence.

or superiority psychosis that ultimately led the Japanese to attack America, resulting in defeat and downfall.

But in the sixth and seventh centuries, when the Old Shinto, formless and somewhat inchoate, was being transformed by the civilizing influence of Buddhism, even the imperial family and the aristocracy adopted Buddhism. By the eighth century a process of Buddhist penetration of Shintoism began. The Kami, or gods of Shinto, were discovered by Buddhist priests to be incarnations of Buddhas and Bodhisattvas appearing on the islands of Japan. The Sun Goddess Amaterasu Omikami was found to be a manifestation of Buddha Vairochana. Hachiman, the God of War, and the Bodhisattva Kshitigarbha were found to be identical. Thus developed what is known as Ryobu Shinto, or Mixed Shinto—"The Two-fold Way of the Gods." For perhaps a thousand years the two religions, Buddhism and Shinto, were practiced as one religion.

In 1600, however, a great change came over Japan. The long feudal warfare of clans and chieftains was draining and demoralizing Japan. A family of the name of Tokugawa brought unity into

this chaotic state by establishing the Shogunate or dictatorship that lasted nearly three hundred years (1600 to 1867). For Shinto, it was a period of reaction. Ryobu Shinto had attempted to weld Buddhism, Confucianism and Shinto into one consistent system. Under the Shoguns, however, a revival of Shinto began. Thousands and thousands of Christians (converted by Francis Xavier and others) were slain. The ports of Japan were closed to foreigners for two hundred years.

In the eighteenth century there arose a great scholar, Motoöri, to whom the admixture of Buddhism and other foreign elements in Shinto were an offense. He devoted himself to the old forms of Shinto and wrote a commentary on the *Kojiki* that is still used by scholars and students. His pupil Hirata carried on the work with even more zealous energy. To him, Buddha was admissible into the Shinto pantheon only in a very inferior place. The work of both Motoöri and Hirata contributed markedly to the weakening of the Shogunate and to the restoration of the Mikado in 1868.

Motoöri's ideas would have delighted Hitler. Perhaps they delighted Tojo. The Mikado, he said,

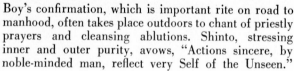

Most violent of Shinto's spring festivals aptly honors Hachiman, God of War. In every city, scores of shoving, strong-armed youngsters carry Mikoshi or tiny shrine containing god's spirit along crowded streets to temple.

→

is a direct descendant of the gods. Japan, briefly, is ruled by a god. It follows that Japan is superior to any other country, since none of the others are ruled by a god or by any offspring of gods. Since no other nation is the equal of Japan, it follows all must pay homage to Japan's sovereign. As to the quality and character of the sovereign, that does not enter into human calculation at all. The ways of gods are inscrutable and past understanding. Whatever the prince does is right. Altogether this was an excellent setup for chauvinism, reaction and, as events proved, aggression.

These doctrines, however, were only one element in hastening the ending of the Shogunate and restoration of the Emperor of Japan to full sovereignty. A most important factor was Commodore Perry, who in 1853 paid a visit to Japan with four gunboats and a message from the President of the United States. The message was a polite request that the ruler of Japan, which was then closed to foreign trade, permit American whaling and other ships to put in there for water and supplies, and open a few ports to foreign trade. No immediate answer was given, and Perry sailed away. He re-

turned the following year with ten ships and 2,000 men, and the answer was yes.

The Shogun had acted on his own. The innocuous Emperor now asserted himself and insisted he must have a hand in the matter. The Shogun finally gave in, abolished his own office and the Emperor was restored to full sovereignty. A process of westernization had begun upon signing the treaty with America and that even the return of the divine Emperor could not halt. Japan began its second and most tremendous transformation. It determined to become as militarily strong and as modern industrially as any of the Western powers.

With the support of the feudal lords, heads of the clans that had been instrumental in the restoration, unity of religion and government were not only revived but reinforced. A government Department of Shrines was established. By the year 1872, Shinto was officially taught in the schools. "Obedience to the gods" was the central tenet, and the visible god on earth was 'the Emperor. The Department of Shrines was later divided into a Bureau of Shinto Shrines, under the Department of Home Affairs, and a Bureau of Reli-

Purification of priests and laity by washing hands precedes worship in any sectarian shrine. In courtyard of Kyoto church, head priest and attendants wash before entering prayer hall. Service, which includes ritual and meditation, is climaxed by sermon centering on such topics as benevolence, courage and wisdom as highest virtues or nature and God as one. True Shinto is a free religion with few fixed forms or dogmas.

gions, under the Department of Education. The Shinto Shrines were government-supported.

No one who has not spent some time in Japan can easily grasp the various facets of Shinto. There is the "god shelf" in every house where not only ancestors are worshiped and memorials of them kept, but various other sacred images, pictures, relics, a stone, a mirror, a string of beads, anything concrete that betokens the presence of the god. These are called *shintai*. Any people that has been more or less homogeneous for a long time develops a set of folk beliefs which, in the course of ages, become virtually compulsive. Even animals are worshiped, as the fox, messenger of the Goddess Inari. She is worshiped as the Kami of Rice and as the deity of geishas and courtesans. The phallic symbols along the roadside, the spirits of trees and mountains, all are part of the popular Shinto that pervades Japan.

The *Shua Shinto*, that is sectarian Shinto, is of a far more religious texture, primitive though it is. There are perhaps a dozen different sects, and for the most part theirs are eclectic beliefs, some influenced by Confucianism, some by Hindu Yogism, and some, like the Tenri Kyo, by Christian Science. Out of these may eventually come a religion with the elements of enlightenment and universalism inherent in the good-will religions.

But the State Shrines, government-supported, became the god-houses most favored. The shrine usually stands upon high ground in a grove among pines and cryptomerias, those magnificent conifers that rise to eighty, ninety and even a hundred feet. At the entrance stands the *torii* with the upward-turning curved ends of the crossbar. A worshiper stopped at a fountain before approaching the shrine, dipped his hands and rinsed his mouth as a purification. Then he bowed to the shrine, clapped his hands, rang the bell hanging from the eaves, left an offering in a box, prayed, bowed with great reverence and departed. All this before the outer shrine. Beyond it stood the inner sanctuary. That was not entered by the worshiper. It contained the *shintai*, some object connected with the god of the shrine, a mirror, a sword, a bit of writing, or a crystal ball.

At the great shrines, the essentials are the same, but more awe-inspiring, or perhaps one should say gloom-inspiring. Many, if not most foreign visitors to Japan make the journey to Nikko, one of the oldest shrines in Japan. It is only ninety-one miles from Tokyo, and its scenery, always allowing for the somber quality of Japanese scenery, is imposing. A magnificent avenue of cryptomerias leads to and through the town, to the famous red-lacquered, curved bridge we so often see in colored prints of Japan. That bridge, for foot traffic only, leads to the park of the shrines. A number of temples form the group. Only certain ones may be visited, and none without removing one's shoes before entering. The all but forbidding cleanliness, the chill, austere polish of floors and doors may inspire awe, but devotion seems to freeze with the marrow in one's bones. Temple dancers at some of the shrines show a willingness to dance for any who will encourage them.

But the most sacred and the most honored of all shrines in Shinto is the shrine at Isé, situated on the main island, on the shore of the Inland Sea. Dedicated to the Sun Goddess herself, that shrine is identified with the origin of the Japanese state and her government. Here, four miles of shrines connect the shrine of Amaterasu with that of Toyo-Uke-Hime, the Food Goddess. The shrine of the Sun Goddess, the Inner Shrine, contains those immemorial imperial regalia which the goddess sent down from Heaven by her grandson, Ninigi—the mirror, the sword and the stone beads.

There were certain fixed state ceremonies at Isé and at certain other important shrines, like the ceremony of purification, a sort of imperial absolution of sins, twice each year. The regular daily worship and prayer, called *norito*, continued without interruption. When a new Emperor was about to mount the throne he worshiped at Isé in person. When war was declared on some foreign power the Emperor, likewise, announced it to the gods, in person, at the Imperial Shrine of Isé.

In religion, it has been said, we have first, symbols and forms; next, mythology; and last, philosophy. In Shinto, only the first two steppingstones have been passed. The third has not yet been

Love of their beautiful land and contemplation of "Heaven-and-Earth-Including Deity" sustaining it is preoccupation of priests. Without formal creed, clergy often marries, owns property, maintains balance between Shinto as national religion and universal faith.

Paying prayerful respect to Japan's war dead, thousands pass daily through *Yasakuni* or Nation-Protecting Temple in Tokyo. A solemn ritual raises heroic dead to rank of gods. Kyoto's shrines (below), which make city fountainhead of Shinto, draw multitude of pilgrims.

reached. Not improbably, one reason why Shinto seems never even to have struggled to reach the Ultimate was the turn it took toward military prowess. Even from earliest times, the Way of the Gods really became the way of the *Samurai*, the way of the warriors. Whatever the elements supplied to Bushido, "the knightly warrior's way," by other religions, such as Zen Buddhism and Confucianism, Shinto supplied the absolute devotion to clan chief, country and Emperor that made it a religious duty. In universal religions, the first duty is to God. In nationalistic Shinto, the first duty is to the Emperor. In 1890 the then Emperor issued a famous rescript on Education which made Shinto both an instrument of policy and an instrument of patriotism. The Yasukuni shrine in Tokyo, which holds the names of all the war dead, became a sort of temple of patriotism. Lest any Japanese should be attracted by Buddhism, Confucianism, or Christianity, one professor announced that Shinto includes them all, that the founders of those other religions were but the missionaries of the god of Shinto. And the Emperor of Japan is that God's vice-regent on earth.

In General MacArthur's report on the "Political Reorientation of Japan," we read on page 467 the now famous memorandum on the "Abolition of Government Sponsorship, Support, Perpetuation, Control, and Dissemination of State Shinto (Kokka Shinto, Jinja Shinto)." It is dated 15 December, 1945. It frees the Japanese from the state-imposed form of Shinto, assures them of complete religious freedom and promises Sect Shinto and Shrine Shinto, purged of its militaristic and ultra-nationalist elements, the same protection as all other religions. The myths of superiority must be deleted. In short, at present Shinto is no longer a state religion.

Only a few days after MacArthur's memorandum, on New Year's Day, 1946, the Emperor Hirohito sent this message to his people:

"The ties between Us and Our people have always stood upon mutual trust and affection. They do not depend upon mere legends and myths. *They are not predicated upon the false conception that the emperor is divine and that the Japanese people are superior to other races and are fated to rule the world.*"

We italicize the last lines because they would seem to put an end forever to the Hitlerian doctrine of superiority. They could conceivably be the opening of a way not only to the purification and elevation of Shinto itself, but also to real democracy and real religion.

**WEDDED ROCKS OF ISÉ** are part of Japan's famous shrine where faithful worship Amaterasu, ancestral Sun Goddess who founded Japanese empire. Today, she is worshiped as divine spirit behind nature, life, religion.

→

Scenic Nara Park, covering 1,250 acres and containing awesome array of temples, museums and statues, is sacred to Shintoists and Buddhists. *Goju-no-To* or five-storied pagoda (above) represents elements of earth, water, fire, air and sky and is typical of Nara's memorial towers. This combination of natural and artistic beauty inspires devout to belief, "In even a single leaf of tree, the awe-inspiring Deity manifests itself."

**GLITTERING JAINA TEMPLE** in Calcutta, with its marble pillars, jeweled inlays, polished mirrors, is one of world's beautiful buildings. Highly ethical sect, which split from Hinduism in 6th century B.C., now numbers 1,500,000.

# 6. JAINISM AND SIKHISM

*Non-injury is the highest religion because the unseen*
*God dwelleth in everything and shineth in every heart*

O ABRAHAM LINCOLN IS attributed the saying that God must love the poor because he has made so many of them. On the same principle God must love sects and creeds because their number is so great. One would hesitate to say how many thousands of sects the combined religions of the world could muster. Some of the sects, as we know, become independent religions. How radically some of them differ from others! Yet all religions are so many paths to God. Consider Jainism, the creed that will not kill a gnat, and Sikhism, that permits meat eating and praises the sword. Yet both are vital religions in India today, with millions of followers.

### 1. *The Religion of Non-Injury*

The founder of Jainism was Mahavira, meaning "the great hero." He was called a "Jina," a conqueror, because he had conquered himself. In the India of the sixth century B.C. that was regarded as the greatest of conquests.

Carrying lances as well as knives, Sikh merchants walk to work in Holy City of Amritsar. Sikhism changed from quietist faith to religion of sword under Islamic persecution in 17th century. Today, with martial fervor diverted, they are noted for devotion to One True God.

He was born almost forty years before Buddha —in 599 B.C.—and, according to the Indian institution of caste, he was a Kshatriya. That is, the caste next to the Brahmin. To it belong kings, princes, chieftains, generals, warriors of all sorts. Siddhartha, a man high in his state, married the Kshatriya lady, Trishala, daughter of a king. As is likely to be the case with a mother who is about to bear a religious founder, Trishala began to be visited by a series of dreams that foretold her son's greatness. Fourteen dreams was the number, and each was indicative of the divine event. All Jaina mothers of great saints have annunciatory dreams.

Trishala dreamed of a great white elephant and a white bull about whom there are some highly poetical remarks. That meant the man to be born would be strong enough to bear the yoke of religion. She dreamed of a bear, of Lakshmi, a goddess of wealth—so many Hindu women have the name of Lakshmi or Shri. She also had dreams of a garland of flowers, of the white moon, the radiant sun and at least seven other highly delightful dreams. In any case, the parents felt assured that the babe to be born would be either a great king or a *Tirthankara*, a pilot to guide humanity across the troubled stream of life to the other shore. He was duly born, and such was the number of legends clustering about his birth that many in later ages believed he was himself a legend and a myth. European scholars, however, have proved the historicity of his existence. As a boy he stopped a mad elephant in his tracks. When he was playing with other children a god appeared and carried him high into the sky, but failed to frighten him. At any rate, he later married a lady named Yashoda, had a daughter named Anuja and, after his parents died, in his thirty-first year, he took up the life of a wandering ascetic, much as did Gautama, the Buddha.

In the West, a man occasionally leaves home to escape a wife. Mahavira and many another Hindu ascetic left home to escape life. Believing as they do in reincarnation, the endless round of rebirths seems terrifying to the Hindus. The great yearning is to liquidate the debts of Karma accumulated in past lives, achieve Nirvana and end forever the ceaseless round of birth and death. When Mahavira renounced the world, sometime in 570 or 569 B.C. his family was supporting an order of monks, and into that order Mahavira was initiated. It is the custom of Hindu Sanyasins to shave off their hair, but the Jaina ascetics tore theirs out by the roots. It is considered as a sign that henceforth the body is negligible. One of the divisions of the Jains, the *Digambara,* or sky-clad ones, wore no clothes at all, to show the uttermost poverty. In our own day that nakedness is somewhat modified. Mohandas K. Gandhi's loincloth was a sop to modern convention from one at heart a Digambara. The other division of the Jains, the *Shvetambara* (what would a religion be without divisions and sects?), believe that Mahavira wore clothes for at least thirteen months after his initiation. Their name, Shvetambara, means the white-clad ones. They wear clothes. For twelve years the ex-prince, Mahavira, wandered from place to place as a mendicant monk, never staying longer than a single night in a village, or more than five nights in a town. That was to prevent forming friendships or habits that could spell temptation. Sin could find no place in him. Renounce! Renounce! That is the silent slogan reverberating in the mind of the ascetic. Possessions, attachments, are insuperable obstacles to enlightenment.

While seated under a spreading Sala tree in a field near an old temple one day, in the thirteenth year of his wandering life, supreme knowledge came to Mahavira, "complete and full," the knowledge called *Kevala jnana.* It was then he became a Jina, a conqueror of Karma, armed with the supreme knowledge that is the property of Teachers of men. What was the great message Mahavira now had to impart? It was this, according to the Jains:

"Birth is nothing and caste is nothing, but Karma is everything."

Only by way of asceticism, Mahavira held, by the practice of austerities, could one consume all one's past Karma and emerge a Tirthankara.

Next to asceticism as a means of cleansing his soul, Mahavira's strongest conviction was that of *ahimsa,* non-injury to any living being whatsoever. To undertake *ahimsa* anywhere is difficult enough. To undertake it in tropical India, which is simply teeming with life, is stupendous. He never walked during the monsoon, or rainy season, because the paths and roads were literally crawling with life. He had his eyes fixed directly before him on an oblong space "the length of a man," so as to avoid stepping on the slightest living thing. Any insect life upon his body enjoyed a field day, for he never scratched or molested it. He swept the ground of any spot he meant to sleep on, and in his begging bowl accepted only left-overs of food prepared for other mouths. Let no life, not even the life of a leek or eggplant, be taken on *his* account.

His first disciples were kings and warriors, his own kinsfolk and caste. Today most of the Jains

Squatting barefoot with their swords, *Singhs,* or "Lions," rest in square before entering Golden Temple to worship. Despite military trappings and stalwart physiques, Sikhs who number 6,000,000 in India heed Prophet Nanak, "Fight with no weapon but word of God."

Every 12 years, observance of *Mahamastakabhisheka* or "great head-anointing ceremony" draws thousands of Jains to Mysore in South India for one of greatest religious festivals on earth. Breath-taking object of their pilgrimage (below) is 57-foot granite colossus of Jaina saint, Gomateswara (above), which has watched over India for 1,000 years. The festival's climax comes when, after two weeks of ceremony, selected priests and pilgrims pour 1,008 pots of milk, curds and sandal paste over statue's giant head (left). Jaina saint, whose spiritual absorption is depicted in huge monolith, taught non-injury to all life, indestructibility of the soul.

are middle-class people, merchants, bankers, money-lenders. Neither these nor the aristocrats were Brahmins, which would lend some color to the belief that Jainism was a revolt against Brahmanism. It is claimed that in the thirty years of his preaching, Mahavira converted many Indian states, and many a king and chieftain entered his order. There were fourteen thousand monks and nuns of Jaina at the time of his passing. Many a rainy season was spent in Vaishali, the place of his birth, and there he was a prophet honored in his own country. For he was the brother of the king.

Among the numerous legends that always cluster round the death of a saint who believes he has conquered death, those pertaining to Mahavira are glowing. One tells how he preached for six days on end to all the rulers of the country. On the seventh day, he took his seat on a diamond throne especially built for him, in a great hall. The night was dark, but the many gods and divine beings gathered to hear the Tirthankara illumined the place with their supernatural glow. He assumed the canonical position, crossed legs and folded hands, and just as dawn was breaking he passed into Nirvana, to be born on earth no more. The layers of Karma every human being is heir to were now for him exhausted.

Mahavira's teaching is elaborate, and is set down in a voluminous scriptural literature. The first of those scriptures are the Eleven *Angas* and the Fourteen *Puranas*. Five points in that creed are regarded as of supreme importance. They are embodied in the Five Great Vows that must be taken by all ascetics.

The first vow runs: I renounce all killing of living beings, whether movable or immovable. Nor shall I myself kill living beings, nor cause others to do it, nor consent to it. Such is the great vow of *ahimsa*, harmlessness, non-injury.

In the second vow, against untruthfulness, the monk or nun undertakes to speak only what is "pleasant, wholesome and true." Truth, it is explained, is untruth if it is not pleasant and wholesome.

The third vow is against stealing or taking or using anything not freely given or permitted.

Fourth is the vow of chastity. Without celibacy none can be a religious at all. *Brahamacharya*, as it is called, is the key to monastic life. Monks are told they must not even talk about a woman, or look at her, or even recall the amusement and pleasure women afforded them when they lived in the world.

The fifth is the vow of renunciation, giving up

Beautifully gowned women (above) whisper before devotions in Golden Temple where bearded Guru (below) reads from Noble Book. Sikhs, who borrowed from Hindus and Moslems, defied caste system, elevated women and marriage, exalted the greatness of God.

Great Golden Temple at Amritsar, or Lake of Nectar, is sacred to Sikhs from Bombay to British Columbia. Approached by marble causeway and located in center of 200-foot pool, white marble, gold-domed sanctuary is a shining monument to Indians' religious zeal. Warrior disciple bathes in waters with dagger in turban.

Sikh soldiers, who have served British Empire around world, parade military band in Singapore. Sikhism, originating in India and spreading rapidly today, abhors superstition, upholds the brotherhood of man.

all attachment, all love, for any person or thing. "I renounce all attachments," vows the candidate, "whether to little or much, small or great, living or lifeless things, neither shall I myself form such attachments, nor cause others to do so, nor consent to their doing so."

No religion is more insistent upon inward and outward austerity. The Jains believe in austerity and in taking vows to carry it out. Even non-Jains believe in those vows. When Mohandas K. Gandhi first left his Indian home to study in England, his mother, herself a follower of Vishnu, made her son vow before a Jaina holy man, or *sadhu*, that he would abstain from wine, meat and women.

For a lay brother or sister, there are twelve vows. These can be taken only after a degree of spiritual progress has been made. Certain faults, five of them, have first to be renounced: no more doubts, no desire to belong to another faith, no questioning about the reality of the fruits of Karma, never to praise hypocrites, nor ever to associate with them. Once the postulant answers those demands satisfactorily, he may proceed to take the twelve vows. (1) Never take life intentionally. This eliminates not only such trades as butchering or fishing, but even tilling the soil. That is why most Jains are merchants, lawyers, bankers or moneylenders. (2) Never lie, (3) never steal, (4) maintain purity of body, (5) shun greed, (6) avoid temptation, (7) limit number of things owned or used, (8) be on guard against avoidable evils, (9) set aside fixed periods for meditation, (10) keep periods of self-denial, (11) spend days from time to time as a monk and (12) give alms and support ascetics.

The third of the five faults, which relates to questioning the reality of the fruits of Karma, may need some explanation. The Jaina idea of Karma is perhaps more concrete than it is in either Hinduism or Buddhism. In Buddhism it is described as:

> A round of Karma and of fruit;
> The fruit from Karma doth arise,
> From Karma then rebirth doth spring;
> And thus the world rolls on and on.

To the Jains, the deeds that we do in our various lives do not merely register in some ethereal way, but they leave a veritable deposit on the soul, layer upon layer, until they create a sheath about the soul, several sheaths, as many as five. This, they say, is a real material, subtle but poisonous, and must be got rid of, at any cost.

And though laymen are not monks, they, too, can annihilate old Karmas by ethical conduct and ceaseless vigilance. Non-injury, constant avoidance of bad emotions, like anger, greed, untruth, constant encouraging of the good emotions, goodness, self-control, saintliness—these are important ways of annihilating Karma. The vows are a great help in following such a program. So are the Three Jewels—somewhat reminiscent of elements in the Buddhist Eightfold Path. Right Knowledge, Right Faith and Right Conduct are the jewels. In practicing these one must be on guard against the Three Evil Darts: Intrigue or Fraud, False Belief, Covetousness. And what is the aim of all this vigilant asceticism? The aim is to attain *moksha*, liberation, liberation from death, liberation from birth, forevermore.

In India proper today, there are probably more Jains than Buddhists. Their number is about 1,500,000. The Jaina savior, Mahavira, left a powerful impress upon his followers. And just as Gautama the Buddha was said to be the latest of a series of Buddhas, so Mahavira, the Tirthankara, was declared to be the twenty-fourth of a series of Tirthankaras. Names were found for twenty-three predecessors, and many of them have had temples erected in their honor. The Jaina temples in various parts of India are among that subcontinent's architectural glories.

The whole teaching is based upon asceticism leading toward delivery from birth and death, that is, from mundane existence. Its greatest single commandment is *ahimsa*, non-injury. To the Jains, we of the Western lands are stained with the blood of animal murder. The fear of stepping upon and killing some invisible insect may seem to us absurd. Nevertheless, the Jains are the only religious body that tries to extirpate cruelty and that builds hospitals for sick and injured animals.

## 2. The Sikhs and their Gurus

Everyone has heard of the Sikhs. What is a Sikh? Sikh means "disciple." Sikhs are disciples of a certain prophet or teacher named Nanak, who lived in India about five centuries ago. India has had so many prophets and saints!

But anyone who has traveled in the East and actually seen the Sikhs is at once attracted by information about them. For they are a sightly, impressive folk, bearded, tall, like trees walking. In British possessions and colonies they are, or were, guards and policemen. With their black beards, their white or khaki clothes and turbaned heads, they stood out wherever they happened to be. They are men of authority, men of faith.

In Tien-Tsin, northern China, the writers recall seeing a Sikh policeman directing traffic in the British Concession. The Chinese are seldom tall. But even the Europeans and Americans seemed a smaller race when the bearded Sikh at the crossing towered above them. In his eyes was a look at once benevolent, shrewd and authoritative. Not that all Sikhs are tall and handsome. There are about six million of them. But those who bear arms, the Singhs, or "lions," are a body their race may be proud of.

To speak of them as a race may sound strange, since they are mostly of Hindu stock. But by virtue of their religion they have actually been molded into what is almost a separate race. A separate race, with a separate religion, and neither the one nor the other has diminished with the years. The father of that race and that religion is Baba Nanak —Father Nanak.

Nanak was born in 1469 in the district of Lahore in the Punjab, northwestern India. No need here to enter into the miracles later ascribed to his birth, as is customary with religious founders. Suffice it that he early displayed an interest in religious matters, even when he was still a schoolboy. He spent much time in study and in associating with holy men. The Punjab forests held many a religious teacher and wandering ascetic. From these he doubtless learned much. His parents were orthodox Hindus and naturally accepted all the rules of caste. But from early youth Nanak protested against the tyranny of caste· and the intransigent authority of the Brahminical priesthood.

The Mohammedans, who had first come into India in the tenth century, were by Nanak's time the dominant power in the Punjab and, indeed, throughout most of India. The stern worship of the one God characteristic of Islam was bound to impress certain Hindu religious men, who wanted to

Jain statues near Jaipur are part of magnificent sculptures comprising artistic Sanghiji Temple dating from 11th century. Word Jain, deriving from Sanskrit root *ji*, means "to conquer" lower passions or false self.

→

Severe piety of Jains, based on their scriptural exhortation to "right belief, right knowledge, right conduct," is renowned throughout Orient. Whether praying with Kandy dancers on Adam's Peak in Ceylon (above) or bowing humbly in thatch-roofed village of Ramgad (below), they demonstrate their faith that "One must worship God, serve the Guru, study the scriptures, control the senses, perform austerities, and give alms."

see the more or less decadent Hinduism about them return to a purer state. One of these was Kabir, born about a generation before Nanak, a saint and poet, who learned from the Moslems to hate idols, to disdain rites and asceticism, to proclaim their worthlessness if they were unaccompanied by sincerity and morality. He denied authority to the Vedas and to any merely barren ritualism. His creed, however, contained elements of both Islam and Hinduism. To this day, there are two sects of his followers, one Hindu and one Moslem. Nanak's creed, likewise, contained elements of both faiths. His father, a merchant and agriculturist, desired Nanak to follow in his footsteps. But at these occupations the son was a failure. He was too much absorbed in holy men, yogis, sufis. A small government job was found for him. He worked at it faithfully, but outside of office hours he, together with a Mohammedan friend, a minstrel named Mardana, sang hymns to the One, his Creator.

One day while wandering in the forest he was taken to God's presence in a vision and there received his charge. "I am with thee," God said to him. "I have made thee happy, and also those who shall take thy name. Go and repeat Mine and cause others to do likewise. Abide uncontaminated in the world. Practice the repetition of My name, charity, ablutions, worship, and meditation." It was after this experience, reminiscent of Zoroaster's and Mohammed's, that Nanak burst into song, and thus began the hymnal known as the *Japji*, the most important section of the Sikh bible, the *Granth Sahib*. This was his song of adoration:

"Unity, Active One, True Name! Actor, Pervader, Fearless, devoid of Enmity, Whom Time and the Ages do not cumber, Self-existent, perceptible Guru—Praise! Pre-eminent Truth, primordial Truth, Truth that is, saith Nanak, and will abide forever."

That song is the preamble to a series of thirty-eight hymns that form the most sacred part of Sikh scripture. Nanak was thenceforth the True Name's Guru, the Guru, or Teacher, of the true religion. His first announcement to the people was, "There is no Hindu, nor is there a Musalman, but only brethren under God." It was a great discovery. How often it has been made! But every time it is new, fresh from the opened Heaven. To proclaim that discovery, Nanak began a wandering life that led him all over India. Every soul must be converted to that saving creed of brotherhood.

Together with his minstrel, Mardana, who accompanied the hymnal songs on a stringed instrument called the rebeck, the prophet visited all the chief places of Hindu pilgrimage, Benares, Delhi, Hardwar, the temple of Jagganath, many of the numberless holy places, preaching the True Name. He went, it is said, as far south as Ceylon, as far to the north and west as the Khyber Pass, into Afghanistan, and even reached Mecca. One of the stories told about Nanak is that in the holy Arab city he lay down to sleep with his feet toward the Kaaba. An Arab *imam* rudely kicked him and said, "Who is this sleeping infidel? Why, O sinner, hast thou turned thy feet toward God?" The Guru of the Sikhs replied, "Turn my feet in the direction in which God is not!" He is said to have summarized his teaching thus: "I have appeared in this age to indicate the way unto men. I reject all sects and know only one God, whom I recognize in the earth, the heavens and in all directions."

His minstrel, Mardana, fell ill and died. The many years of homeless wandering told not only on the rebeck player, but on the prophet as well. Nanak was now sixty-nine years old. He knew that death was not far off. He was resolved not to leave his followers without a guide. He would not appoint his sons—he deemed them unworthy. So he appointed his favorite disciple, Angad, who thus became second in a long line of Sikh Gurus. Nanak died in October, 1538. Both Hindus and Moslems among his converts claimed his body for disposal, the one by cremation, the other by interment. Legend says that Nanak's instructions were: "Let the Hindus place flowers on my right, and the Moslems on my left. They whose flowers remained fresh in the morning shall have the disposal of my body." In the morning the flowers on both sides were fresh, but there was no body.

Whether his following was numerous or not was unknown to Nanak when he died. Nor could he tell whether it would go on. He left behind no very definite organization. What he did leave was the *Japji*, thirty-eight psalms, a "book of praise in remembrance of the Lord." Every Sikh knows those 400 lines by heart. Every morning the faithful silently repeat them. It is a simple doctrine they present. The one and only God, the Creator of all things—Nanak calls Him the True Name—He is Sovereign. He manifests himself in numberless ways, in countless places. He predestines and assigns the lot of his creatures. Man is the highest of them, to be served by the others. (Thus meat-eating was interpreted as a legitimate service by the lower creations.)

All created things and beings form a veil of illusion, the Maya of the Hindu religion, including even the various gods, as Brahma, Vishnu and

Sikh husband and wife worship in ornate interior of Patiala Shrine. Reading of sacred scriptures, *Granth Sahib*, praise of God in prayer and hymn, practice of good works are important daily disciplines. "By obeying Him," says Baba Nanak, "man attaineth salvation."

Shiva. "He beholdeth them," said Nanak, "but is not seen by them. This is very marvelous." Yet, "Search not for the True One," charged the Guru. "He is in every heart, and is known by the Guru's instruction." As to pilgrimages, rites, idols, so characteristic of his Hindu environment, how, he asked, could God be contained in an image of wood or stone? On the whole, Nanak taught a quiet, home-loving, almost contemplative, creed. It became its destiny to produce a militant body of some of the finest troops in the Orient.

The first three successors to Nanak followed the quietistic pattern of life suggested by Nanak's teaching. Angad, the immediate successor, modified the Punjabi alphabet and thus created a new one, Guru-Mukhi, in which the sacred writings of the Sikhs were thenceforth recorded. Amar Das, who followed Angad in 1552, is remembered chiefly for his great humility. His successor, Ram Das, excavated further Amritsar (the lake of nectar) in which stands the Durbar Sahib, the Golden Temple, foremost shrine of the Sikhs. It was Guru Arjan, son and successor of Ram Das, who made Amritsar the central home of Sikhism. His term coincided to an extent with that of the great Mogul emperor Akbar (1556-1605), and he seems to have caught some of the energy and magnificence of the most liberal of the Moguls. The Guru assembled all scriptures that made up the *Granth Sahib*, and even wrote a psalm on peace of mind.

Akbar, who was intensely interested in other people's religions and even dreamed of a universal religion, took the time to investigate this new creed. Some of his advisers complained that it slighted Islam. He examined the Granth, the Sikh bible, and announced that he had no fault to find with it. He paid Arjan a visit of state, and that silenced slanderous tongues. But unfortunately, wise fathers are often succeeded by vile sons. The successor to the Mogul throne, Jehangir, arrested Guru Arjan and put him to death. To his son, Har Govind, Arjan left the advice to sit fully armed on his throne and keep as large an army as possible. The Sikhs were now not merely a creed, but a military power.

Guru Har Govind took his father's injunction literally. He created for himself a Sikh bodyguard that at need could give a good account of itself. There was a treasury in the Golden Temple against emergencies. It could not be used to better purpose, the Guru decided, than for the Sikhs to defend themselves. Clothing, rations, weapons, these were the things the treasury provided. The Guru wrote hymns and trained his army. "I bow to God," ran one of

Masked monk (left) wears mouth band to keep from injuring even insects. Jaina holy men, who practice austere maxim, "Harmlessness is the only religion," walk about country barefoot, beg their food, everywhere teach gospel, "Love conquers all." Beggars (right) line steps of Meenakshi Temple at Madura during *Ashtami Chappra* festival. Jains and Sikhs, like orthodox Hindus, recognize begging as honorable profession, give alms in this world to attain the next.

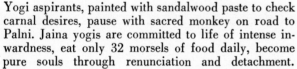

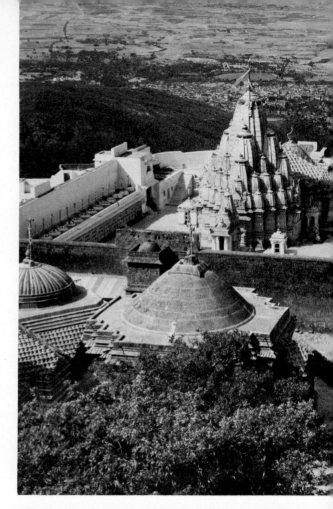

Yogi aspirants, painted with sandalwood paste to check carnal desires, pause with sacred monkey on road to Palni. Jaina yogis are committed to life of intense inwardness, eat only 32 morsels of food daily, become pure souls through renunciation and detachment.

High on Mount Girnar in Junagad State stand the 16 magnificent temples regarded as Mecca of Jainism. Second only to Benares as a place of pilgrimage, *Deva Kota* or Abode of the Gods soars 2,370 feet above Indian plains, dates back to 12th century. As Jainism

his hymns, but in the very next line he added, "I bow to the Scimitar, the two-edged sword." He trusted in God and kept his powder dry.

The bowing to the two-edged sword was not mere poetry. One day, during the great April festival in honor of the goddess Durga, the *shakti*, or feminine aspect of Hindu divinity, when many Sikhs were assembled, Govind drew his father's sword from its scabbard, held it high and demanded to know who would be willing to give his life for the sake of Sikhism. There was no answer. Durga, he explained, required actual blood sacrifice if their cause was to succeed. Durga is not a Sikh divinity, but a Hindu folk goddess, Kali, the Mother. Slowly, five men rose and made their way forward. Govind took each of the five into his tent and came forth after each one with his sword dripping with blood. The bystanders were awe-stricken. Some fled in mortal terror. Soon, however, Govind called to the presumed "dead" men, one by one, and they came out of the tent. The blood on the sword blade was

goat's blood. It had been a terrible test of faith.

What Govind needed and wished to create was an elite, a chosen body, a *Khalsa*, as he said, whose meaning is purity, devotion. By a simple ceremony he "baptized" the five, and they in turn baptized him. He gave them as a slogan, or battle cry: "*Wah Guruji ka Khalsa!* Hail, the Khalsa of the Guru. *Wah Guruji ki Fatah!* Hail the victory of the Guru!" That cry has since been heard on many a battlefield. The baptized ones baptized others. Those initiates had a new name added to their own: *Singh*, or Lion. They must always wear the five K's: the *Kes*, long hair and beard. The *Kangha*, or comb. The *Kachk*, or short drawers, hence the word khaki. *Kara*, a steel bracelet on their arms. *Khanda*, a steel dagger. Alcohol and tobacco were forsworn, but a diet of meat was encouraged. Thousands flocked to join the order. It became a growing army. Caste did not obtain. Even pariahs and untouchables were taken in as equals. Under the new discipline and the new diet they were all welded

itself shows the influence of Buddhist reverence for life, so its architecture adopted style of Buddhist stupas. Tall temples, which have such names as Vastupala and Tramprati, are center of occultism where many masters have ascended to full God-consciousness.

Mothers and children, visting Jaina temple at twilight, typify average family's ceaseless attention to life of the spirit. Together, in loving worship, they repeat Hindu prayer, "O God, lead me from darkness to light, from unreal to real, from death to immortality."

into stalwart soldiers of an excellent army. Their armor was purity of living and faith in their Gurus and their God.

This does not mean that all Sikhs were thenceforth Singhs. But it does mean that the Khalsa now formed the powerful backbone of the sect. They continued to have their troubles with the Moslem power, encountering defeat now and then. In 1708 the Guru, Govind Singh, was stabbed by a Moslem. He was the last of the Gurus. His two sons perished in these wars with the Moslems. None succeeded Govind. He provided that henceforth the Granth itself, the sacred scripture, should be the Guru. It contained all the knowledge, leadership and teaching the Sikhs might need. And it has worked.

The Khalsa brought the Sikhs a solidarity which many a greater, non-theocratic state might envy. Their religious center is the Golden Temple at Amritsar, where the Granth is daily reverenced. The political headquarters are at Lahore. For a time the Sikhs were the real power over the entire

Punjab. They fought the British when they came, but were defeated under Dhulip Singh, the last Sikh ruler, in 1849, and in token of their good faith presented Queen Victoria with the virtually priceless diamond, the Kohinoor. When the mutiny broke out in India, in 1857, the Sikhs confirmed their loyalty pledge by flocking to the British colors and helping to save India and British prestige.

Since World War II, they have been agitating to have a state of their own. As it is, their homeland is divided between Pakistan and India. Amritsar is assigned to India. The Sikhs feel themselves torn. Both Pakistan and India have promised them religious freedom and full liberty. But the Sikhs, who are a proud people, feel entitled to their own state.

The last words of Nanak's psalms, the *Japji*, declare:

> Salvation comes at last to those whose
> thought rests on the Name.
> Their faces glow, saith Nanak, and they
> have become immortal.

# 7. ZOROASTRIANISM
## *Good thoughts, words, deeds, and the wise Lord, Ahura Mazda*

OVER AND OVER AGAIN, WE ARE struck by the powerful drive of the great Teachers that will not let them rest. In the face of constant discouragement, of insuperable obstacles, they go on proclaiming their discovery that man is nearer divinity than he realizes. The burning sense of mission within them, the urge to make known the good tidings, leads them to cry out, even to deaf ears, that creation is based in spirit, that God is one, that there are ways of coming closer to Him.

Zoroaster, as we call him, Zarathushtra as the ancient Persians called him, was such a prophet of good news, whom his people at first heeded not at all. It took him ten years to gain his first convert, and that convert was his own cousin. For the very reason, doubtless, that he brought to his people something they had never heard before, he met with coldness, ridicule and rebuff. For a prophet, honor in his own country, and especially in his own town, comes hard. Nevertheless, when he finally accomplished his mission, he became known, and to this day is known, as one of the greatest prophets the earth has produced.

The date of his birth is uncertain. Modern scholars generally accept 660 B.C. as the year. Zoroastrians, as represented by the Parsis of today, incline to the year 1000, or even 1200 B.C. As to the place of his birth, Azerbaijan in northwestern Persia, close to the Armenian border, is believed to have been his cradle. The number of birth legends, characteristic of genealogies of great prophets, is as generous as might be expected. A star appeared, the earth trembled, the universe thrilled with gladness. Nor were the demons idle. Their worst enemy was about to enter the theater of activity where demons can do the most harm and suffer the most damage—this earth. They tried to prevent his birth, to choke the life out of him at the very moment of delivery. It availed them nothing. A heavenly light shone round the house. A cry of joy heralded the birth of a living child. Not only that, but the infant no sooner breathed his first breath than he uttered a loud laugh of triumph that astonished everyone.

The demons, needless to say, did not leave it there. Numerous attempts were made on the life of the child, Zoroaster. While still in the cradle he came near having his head crushed. A herd of cattle would surely have trampled the infant, but that the leading ox took a stance over the boy and saved

Zoroaster, Persia's noble prophet who was born about 660 B.C. and who taught that righteousness is the highest good, believed in a God of Truth and Law.

At Yezd, amid desolate sands of Iran's southeastern desert, a modern Persian contemplates the *Dakhmas* or Towers of Silence where Zoroastrians bury their dead. As mother of life the earth is sacred, according to Zoroastrians, and therefore it must not be polluted by anything dead or decaying. Hence, followers of ancient Persia's greatest philosopher still dispose of their dead by placing corpses atop stone towers where they are consumed by vultures and crows, wind and rain. Zoroastrians, who believe in a Lord of goodness and light and who believe they must "work hard and sacrifice themselves for what is liked by God," comprised the dominant faith of Persia until country was conquered by Moslems in 7th century. Today, their world number is less than 150,000. Yet, their influence on other world faiths is still significant.

him. Even wolves protected the babe in their lair and brought in a sheep to suckle him.

Those dangers of infancy past, Zoroaster at the age of seven was placed in the charge of a wise teacher and there, oddly, the story suddenly becomes blank. The formative years, so important in the history of any life, seem to be neglected by those who record the lives of prophets.

Details of the years between fifteen and thirty are almost as meager as those between seven and fifteen. It is recorded, however, that he helped distribute food to the poor and to animals in time of famine. These were clearly years of religious preparation, and there is a legend that Zoroaster kept silent for seven years. It was also told that he lived in desert places and upon a mountain, illumined by a supernal light, where he communed with his God, Ahura Mazda. At the age of thirty came the Revelation that made of the solitary wanderer one of the world's great prophets. Assumed to be 630 B.C., it is known as "the Year of the Religion."

It was in this Year of the Religion that the

Revering fire as symbol of God's righteousness, Zoroastrians pay perpetual tribute to this element. Priest, tending holy flame, wears mask to prevent its pollution, while holy men (below) greet dawn's early light with fresh plants and silver cups of water.

archangel, Vohu Manah, or Good Thought, appeared to Zarathushtra in a vision, put him in a trance and led his soul to the highest point, the presence of the Ahura Mazda. It was a tremendous charge Zoroaster received in that first vision, and, in a measure, in the seven subsequent conferences with Ahura Mazda that followed during the next ten years. The Wise Lord—a literal rendering of Ahura Mazda—sent him upon the sternest mission anyone in that region had yet received. He sent Zarathushtra to preach uncompromising righteousness. The elements of that creed were Good Thought, Good Words and Good Deeds. From these, one could deviate only at his mortal peril.

As stern as the climate of Media, Bactria and Persia, with its violent contrasts of heat and cold, was the religion of Zoroaster, which saw the world as a battleground between that constantly struggling pair, Good and Evil. For man there was only one side, the Good. That was the side of Ahura Mazda and of his six aides, Good Thought, Righteousness, Divine Kingdom, Devotion, Perfection and Immortality.

These are really Ahura Mazda's being, not attributes but inherent qualities. Most people, however, find it difficult to understand abstractions. So the qualities became archangels, immortals, called the Amesha Spentas. Arrayed against these principalities of Light was Angra Mainyu, Ahriman, the Lie, supported by the old gods of the animistic age of the Aryans. That was the momentous choice man must make—the powers of Light or the powers of Darkness. There were no halfway measures or compromises. Once man made the choice, it was eternal warfare between him and the Lie. When we consider the idolatry that prevailed in the Near and Middle East at that time, virtually everywhere except among the Hebrews, we understand why Zoroaster looms so large in the story of religions.

After the very first conference with Ahura Mazda and the other Immortals, Zoroaster proceeded at once to carry out Ahura Mazda's charge and began teaching, preaching and prophesying. He appeals first to the heretical priests of the old religion, the Kavis and Karpans, as he called them, to turn to Ahura Mazda. He threatens them with hell-fire when they come to the Bridge of the Accountant at the time of death. But he threatens in vain. They are blind and deaf to the Law.

The Gathas, which form part of the Zoroastrian Bible, the Avesta, contain many instances of the prophet's wrath, anathema and curses called down upon heads of unbelievers. During the seven years after his vision and transport in the presence of

As modern Iranian Government prohibits Zoroastrians from maintaining seminaries and colleges to train their clergy, high priests make the circuit from temple to temple to teach candidates (above). In home service (below) in Kerman, Iran, a family burns incense and lights sacred fire in "worship with devotion of that Divine Power, that Lord who is *Ahura Mazda*, the Giver of all joy, the Architect of all good things."

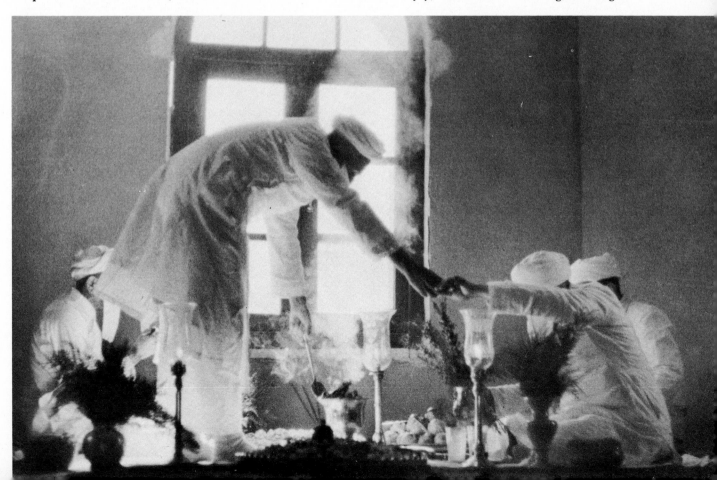

Fabulous city of Persepolis, now a rubble of broken gateways and columns (above), was raised in the 5th century B.C. by Persian monarchs Darius and Xerxes to the glory of the empire and Zoroastrian Ahura Mazda, "the Lord, the creator, the radiant and glorious, the greatest and best." Built near the Mountain of Mercy and dotted with images of Zoroaster, the city's foundation inscription proclaimed: "By the grace of Ahura Mazda, I [Darius] built this fortress. And I built it secure and beautiful and adequate."

Ahura Mazda, he experienced a series of further visions with the archangels. Those six of the heavenly hierarchy were at the very base of the Mazda religion.

Ahura Mazda himself was, of course, the keystone of the arch, the highest—changeless, beneficent, almighty. Apart from him, nothing exists. He is the creator of all things, angels, archangels, men, "the joy-giving cattle," the universe. "He yoked swiftness to wind and clouds." He inspired love between son and father. Weal and woe are by him ordained. He sees into the hearts of men and none can deceive him. The destinies of mortals are in his hands. But how does the changeless Ahura Mazda produce the world of change that we know? He does that by Spenta Mainyu, the Holy Spirit, perhaps, as the King James Bible would put it, the Holy Ghost.

Thus, when Zoroaster, in the high poetic strain of the Book of Job, enquires of Ahura Mazda: "Who determined the paths of suns and stars—who is it by whom the moon waxes and wanes? Who, from below, sustained the earth and the firmament from falling?" There can be only one answer. It is God Himself, Ahura Mazda, by means of Good Mind, Spenta Mainyu, the Holy Spirit, or, as the Greeks might express it, the Logos.

The Greeks, incidentally, entertained a high respect for Zoroaster and his creed. Those who remember Xenophon will recall that the equivalent of the three R's for the Persian boy was to ride, shoot and *speak the truth*. Few contemporary peoples were so concerned for the truth in everyday life. But for the Persian it was natural. Was not Druj, the Lie, the mortal enemy of Ahura Mazda, as well as the mistress of Hell? Druj is a female fiend personifying wickedness in every form. She is the

Stately tomb of Persia's 13th century poet-philosopher Saadi is located at Shiraz. Admired by both Zoroastrian and Moslem, his poetry reflected the Prophet's "best righteousness" and became basis of living Persian language.

→

opposite of Asha, righteousness. The greatest enemy of all is Angra Mainyu, Ahriman, the Evil Spirit, the Evil One.

Never did Ahura Mazda, who is all goodness, create evil, so it must have originated otherwise. Ahriman, the Evil Spirit, who is coexistent with Ahura Mazda, or Ormazd, is its originator. Says the text: "He abode from eternity in the abyss of endless darkness." But the moment the world was created he rushed out bent on destroying it. He is the origin, source and producer of evil and sin. His snake body can assume various and many forms. He is filled with rancor against all creation, because it is Ormazd's. He is the arch-deceiver, beguiling man to wickedness and sin. He produces seductive demons to pervert mankind. He put all the vices in man. It was he—who else?—who introduced disease and death into the world. Snakes, scorpions, lizards, sickness, filth, misery—whose creations could they be but Ahriman's? But the Beast is limited. He has no foreknowledge of what is to be. He is not eternal. When the great Renovation comes and goodness becomes universal, he will be exterminated. His destruction is sure.

There was war between Zoroaster and Angra Mainyu. The prophet embraced Ahura Mazda's side fully, completely. His mission was to make his people and all mankind embrace it. The powerful hierarchy of the good, the great archangels, aspects of Ahura Mazda, made a phalanx of strength on the side of goodness. In the *Gathas*, those Psalms of Zoroastrianism, supposed to be the prophet's own words, he tells how he was called to the good fight. In Yasna 43 of the second Gatha, Zarathushtra recalls:

"As the holy one I recognized thee, Ahura Mazda, when Good Thought came to me and asked me, 'Who art thou? To whom dost thou belong? By what sign wilt thou appoint the days for questioning about thy possessions and thyself?'

"Then I said to him: Zarathushtra am I, a true foe to the Liar, to the utmost of my power, but a powerful support would I be to the Righteous, that I may attain the future things of the infinite Dominion according as I praise and sing thee, Mazdah."

And a powerful support to the righteous he proved to be. Not only was Vohu Manah, Good Thought, on his side, but also Asha, Righteousness, counselor of Ahura Mazda, living in the same abode with Him and Vohu Manah. And just as Vohu Manah is man's ideal, to whom all pray for long life and felicity in his paradisaic realm, and who is also the patron of cattle and the animal world, so Asha, Righteousness, is the giver of long life and counselor of marrying couples, bidding husband and wife to excel each other in pursuing Asha. But Asha requires constant discipline. Purity of body and mind is imperative, and without devotion man runs the risk of spiritual death.

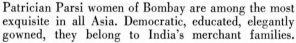

Patrician Parsi women of Bombay are among the most exquisite in all Asia. Democratic, educated, elegantly gowned, they belong to India's merchant families.

Parsis or Persians, in characteristic flowing dress and circular caps, leave Zoroastrian fire temple after Sunday worship. Ancient religion's many parallels with

Then there is Khshathra, sometimes translated Noble Government. It means the divine majesty of Ahura Mazda. The good share in that power. It is the domain of spirituality. Both earthly and spiritual riches are embodied in Khshathra. There are also Armaiti, Devotion—in the Hindu Vedas she is called Aramati—Haurvatat and Ameretat, Perfection and Immortality. These are the reward of good thoughts, good words, good deeds, righteousness and devotion, the basic imperatives of Zoroastrian conduct. Those last two archangels also have charge of water and plants. Good husbandman that he was, Zarathushtra never forgot the farm and its needs.

"What is the thing," he asked, "which gives most pleasure to the earth?"

"When a pure man walks upon her."

"What is the next most pleasurable thing to her?"

"When a pure man builds a house where are cattle and fine flocks, where there is a woman and children. In such a house is abundance and righteousness."

There are numerous other powers, as for instance, Atar, the same as the Hindu Agni, God of Fire. Those Aryan worshipers, long before the Hindus separated from the Iranians, had a very sacred fire cult. In Zoroastrianism it remained so firmly that the religion was early, and mistakenly, called fire worship. Fire never displaced the worship of Ahura Mazda. In Iran, however, there were at least ten noted altars to the sacred fire before Zoroaster. So ingrained in the Iranian mind was the fire cult that Zoroaster incorporated it into his system and puri-

Christianity and Judaism include regular services, strict moral code, resurrection of dead and a Golden Rule, "Do not unto others that which is not good for oneself."

Silk-saried Parsi, strolling Malabar Hill, is descendant of faithful who fled Persia, 1,300 years ago. Today, they have few equals for uprightness and generosity.

fied it. Fire is light, and light is the symbol of Ahura Mazda, and therefore of the Zoroastrian faith. Fire is to play a great part in the Renovation that is to come. "Divine judgment will be meted out to man through the red fire of Mazda."

Up and down Persia went Zarathushtra, trying to persuade his fellow men to embrace that stern creed and earn salvation. They wanted none of him or his creed. Then a break came in the dark cloud of his gloom. In eastern Iran, there was an Aryan prince named Vishtaspa. According to one account, Zarathushtra, so to speak, bearded King Vishtaspa at the race track and began to preach his cult. In another version, the King was seated in state in his palace when the roof suddenly parted and Zoroaster appeared before the throne. In his hand, declares

the Arabian author of this tale, was a cube of fire with which the prophet played without its hurting him.

The King was surrounded by his wise men, the well-entrenched priests of the ancient religion, which the prophet sought to displace. He told Vishtaspa and his court of the power and attributes of Ahura Mazdah, of the archangels that can transform life for the man of good thoughts, good words and good deeds. He told them of the darkness and evil of Ahriman, the Liar, and his myrmidons, the *Daevas*. There he touched a dangerous subject. The Daevas were the gods, the nature gods, of the old religion. Even polytheists don't like their gods described as devils. Our very word devil comes from the Daevas. The priests about Vishtaspa rose in

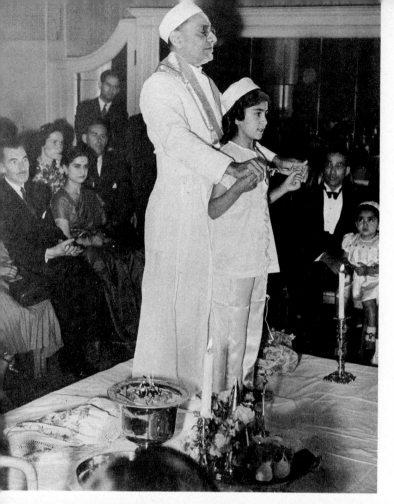

*Naojote* or light-giving service is impressive rite in life of Parsi child. Consecrated into religion of purity and justice, initiate (above) wears white sacred shirt, repeats the Zoroastrian Lord's Prayer beginning, "The will of the Lord is the law of righteousness."

wrath. They would rid the place of this upstart prophet. They literally "framed" him. They had some of the materials of witchcraft placed in his lodgings and had him imprisoned as a wizard, an unholy necromancer.

Then came to pass the miracle that not only released Zarathushtra from prison, but actually brought about the conversion of Vishtaspa. The King had a favorite black horse. No sooner was Zarathushtra imprisoned than that priceless charger suffered a strange collapse. His four legs were suddenly drawn up into his belly and he could not move. News like that traveled rapidly and penetrated even the thick walls of Zoroaster's cell. The messenger of Ahura Mazda was, as we know, an ardent husbandman and a lover of cattle. Besides, he was who he was. He offered to cure the horse and to return it to perfect health—upon certain conditions. The King was eager to accept and gladly promised a special boon to the divine "vet" for each

foot of the beloved horse that is restored to its former health.

The conditions were these: If one foot of the horse was restored, the King was immediately to accept the religion of Ahura Mazda. The prophet uttered a prayer and the thing was done. The second condition was that the King's son, Isfendiar, must fight as a crusader for the new and true faith. Agreed. Promptly, the right hind leg of the steed came out. The third condition was that the Queen, too, must embrace the faith, and there was yet a fourth. The fourth condition was that the conspirators who had plotted against Zoroaster and had him imprisoned must be named and liquidated. No sooner was this accomplished than the horse leaped up on all four legs as sound as in his best days.

Conversion of that Aryan monarch was the great starting point for the spread of the religion of Ahura Mazda. For the entire court soon embraced the new Faith, and the people followed. Two of the king's ministers, Frashaoshtra and Jamnaspa, became family connections of Zoroaster. Frashaoshtra gave the prophet his daughter, Huovi, to wife, while Jamnaspa married Pourocista, Zoroaster's daughter by an earlier marriage.

The twenty years that followed were spent in ceaseless propagation of the Faith throughout the lands of Iran and in fighting holy wars on its behalf. In the first of these, the King's son, Isfendiar, more than made good his father's pledge. He routed the enemy and became a national hero. The second war was less successful. The Turanian invaders penetrated far into Iran, and the prophet himself is said to have met his death in it. In Balkh, where Zoroaster was standing in prayer before a fire altar, a savage Turanian cut him down.

The religion by that time was so solidly based in Iran that it continued to grow by its own momentum. Its monotheistic adherence to Ahura Mazda, its singularly high ethical content and its practical belief in working the soil and husbandry made the foundation of the Faith. It is the good, said Zoroaster, who till the soil, reclaim wasteland, irrigate the barren lands, raise grain and fruit and treat all domestic animals kindly, especially the cow. They lead good domestic lives and they never lie. The evil have no interests like these. They are Daeva worshipers.

The Daevas, those old gods of the Aryans, died hard. For besides the Fire, the ancient Aryan god Mithra remained as a high divinity among the Iranians. He was a war god, a supporter of the sanctity of treaties and a god of personal loyalty.

Smiling happily before mother and Parsi congregation, little Nivaz Mistry sits in lotus posture after ceremony. She is now bound forever to the adoration of Ahura, renunciation of Satan, purity of soul, mind and body.

→

Formal initiation into religion takes place at age 7. In London ceremony, identical with that performed in Bombay or Karachi, Nivaz Mistry becomes a Zoroastrian. Parsi priest Dastur Bode (above and left) be-

gins service by lighting fire and chanting watchword of faith, "I practice good thoughts, good words, good deeds." As keeper of religion, he sprinkles her with rose petals (above), consecrates her soul to "Holy Zoroaster."

Parsi wedding, with bride and groom garlanded with flowers and surrounded by relatives, takes place in bride's home in Bombay. After priests sprinkle them with holy water, they encircle couple seven times with *Kosti* girdle and pray, "May the Wise Lord bless you with many sons, good livelihood and a life of 150 years."

Parsi stress on education, even in such rural sectors as Surat, has made their literacy rate of 74 per cent highest in India. Old schoolmaster (above), walking with his pupils, teaches them from *Avesta* "to exercise liberality; to do justice; to be friendly to everyone; to be sincere and true and shun falsehood."

Mithra rose higher and higher, and in later Zoroastrianism he was the son of Ahura Mazda. He was the God of Light, second only to Ahura Mazda, and the God of Truth, Purity and Honor, the foe of Ahriman and that devil's lies, evil and filth. In the fabric of Aryan myth there was a Primeval Bull. Mithra had slain that Bull and thereby became the creator and fashioner of all earthly beings. So that when the Roman general Pompey's soldiers brought this religion to Rome from the Near East, an artist pictured Mithra as kneeling on the back of a bull and plunging a knife into its neck. That subsequently became the symbol of the creed.

The remarkable thing about Mithraism was its startling parallelism to many of the tenets of Christianity. The seventh day of each week was regarded as sacred to the Sun God (Sunday), and toward the end of December the birth of Mithra was celebrated more or less simultaneously with the winter solstice. The Sun God, that is Mithra, would thenceforth give more and more light. The cult was equipped with a priesthood, with a high pontiff, and celibate and virgin servitors. Worshipers took consecrated bread and wine as in Christian communion, and a bell tolled at the climax of the service. An undying flame was maintained at the entrance to the crypt in which Mithra slew the Bull. The morality and ethical code of

Mithraism was as high as that of Zoroaster. After death all souls must appear before the judgment seat of Mithras (in Zoroastrianism he was one of *three* judges), and the good would rise to Ahura Mazda, while the wicked would be shunted to Ahriman for eternal punishment. During the second and third centuries of our era, Mithraism was a competitor of Christianity. The Church Fathers resented the parallelisms and accused Mithra's cult of plagiarism. But it was Christianity that became the religion of the Roman Empire, and Christianity triumphed.

Altogether, it was a rich religious heritage that Zarathushtra left his people when he departed this world to meet Ahura Mazda. It made Persians a great people and Persia a great empire, until it fell to Alexander the Great. It built solid virtues and rigid disciplines into the character, and for a time the people were invincible. Even the eschatology the prophet bequeathed his followers was stern, uncompromising and new. At the end of the age, that is, the present world order, a general resurrection and a final judgment will take place. The good and the evil will be subjected to an ordeal by fire and molten metal. The evil will be terribly burned, but for the good the liquid metal will be no harsher than warm milk.

The judgment after death is somewhat different.

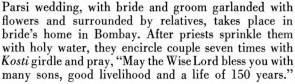

Cyprus and palm trees line 80-step entrance leading into Bombay Towers of Silence. Such burial towers are peculiar to Zoroastrians who consider a corpse's touch defiling, yet who believe "The dead shall rise up."

There, as we have seen, each soul comes to the Bridge of the Accountant or the Separator. That is the dread Chinvat Bridge. This bridge, though it spans the Abyss of Hell, has an entrance to Paradise at its farther end. So near to each other are the two extremes. The bridge itself sounds almost like some giant scale. Depending on which cup predominates, the record will indicate the way. If good, a hand will point toward Paradise at the end of the bridge. If evil, the sinner will be unable to go on. The heavy burden of sin and guilt consciousness will pull him down into the abyss below. In other words, Zoroaster discovered what we have been discovering ever since, namely, that character is destiny.

There is some doubt as to precisely when Zoroastrianism began. But by the time Persia was a great empire, capable of overthrowing Babylon and the Chaldean empire, the religion of Ahura Mazda was the official religion of the Persian emperors, of Cyrus the Great, Darius, Xerxes and the rest. In time, however, changes and modifications creep into every religion. Mahayana Buddhism transformed the primitive and sterner Hinayana. The religion of the Upanishads succeeded that of the vedic period. The Taoism of longevity pills and life elixirs followed the high concepts of the Tao Teh King. Similarly, the Zoroastrianism of the Persian Empire was no longer quite the religion of Zoroaster.

For one thing, Zoroaster himself was virtually deified, and that stern prophet of sober virtue and good husbandry was worshiped almost like a god. All manner of supernatural phenomena were credited to his birth and life. Somehow the "Glory of Ahura Mazda," a sort of holy ghost, united itself with the future mother of Zoroaster at *her* birth and thus prepared the steps for a kind of immaculate conception.

Then there was the rise and power of the Magi. They were not a sect or a group so much as a tribe. They were known before Zoroaster and, according to some authorities, opposed to him at first. But later they embraced his creed and became its priests. They were widely known for their skill in magical arts, divination, astrology and the like, to the Greek world and even as far as Jerusalem. There is a tradition that Pythagoras had studied with them in Babylon and, later, Plato was just about to journey to them when the Graeco-Persian

War broke out and prevented it. They became more and more influential and later recognized as the best-known exponents of Zoroastrianism in the Near and Middle East. The legend of their coming to visit Mary at the time of the birth of Jesus is in itself a proof of their fame and influence.

Many of the changes in Zoroastrianism took place during the great prosperity of Persia which existed chiefly under the Achaeminian kings, from Cyrus the Great (558-528 B.C.), conqueror of Babylon, to Darius III (336-330), whom Alexander the Great conquered. There was a sort of revival under the Sassanian Kings (A.D. 226-651) until the Persian power was finally snuffed out by the conquering Moslems in the middle of the seventh century A.D. After that, only remnants of Zoroastrians remained. Today there are said to be no more than 150,000 in the world, with the majority, under the name of Parsis, concentrated in Bombay, India, to which land many of them emigrated. In other parts of India and in Persia itself, there is a scattering of small communities. The notable fact, however, is that the Mazdayasnian religion survives at all.

That, however, is not the chief reason Zoroastrianism looms so imposingly in the history of religions. The great force and purity of spirit of its prophet, and his Revelation coming as early as it did, makes it outstanding in the world's history. Then there are the many parallelisms with Judaism and Christianity, which bring it close to our Western faiths. First of all it is a monotheism. Ahriman, the prince of darkness and lies and all evil, is the prototype of Satan, whom the Jews, according to most scholars, adopted from the Persians. His characteristics and activities are very similar in all three faiths. Also, the doctrine of a future life, with a system of rewards and punishments, with an elaborate description of life in the Hereafter, was taught by Zarathushtra ages before the Jews. The Jewish Sheol, prior to Zarathushtra, was as dim and colorless as the Homeric Hades. The whole plan of the Last Judgment seems to have come from Persian into Jewish and, later, into Christian eschatology.

As to the contact of Judaism with the later Zoroastrianism, it is assumed that after Cyrus the Great conquered Babylon in the middle of the sixth century B.C., he found the Jews captive there and immediately liberated them. That created a warm bond between the peoples. At least one great English scholar, the late Dr. James Hope Moulton, believes "there are no adequate grounds for belief in Jewish indebtedness to the Avesta." Most scholars, however, agree that all three religions, Judaism, Christianity and Islam, were influenced by Zoroastrianism.

The Zoroastrians of today, the Parsis, are scattered among their many settlements in India and Persia and in Karachi, the capital of Pakistan. They are a people highly educated, excellent businessmen and exceptionally clean. Two buildings are necessary for every community of Parsis. One is a fire temple, the other a Tower of Silence. The veneration for the element of fire has given rise to the erroneous designation of those people as fire worshipers. Says the great Persian poem, the Shahnameh, "Do not say that they were fire-worshipers; for they were worshipers of God the Holy." Fire is the symbol of Ahura Mazda, and once lighted the fire is kept burning without interruption.

Most Parsis visit the fire temples at least four times a month, though religious people attend almost daily. The prayers recited before the sacred fire are whatever the worshiper pleases. Usually, however, they are the *Kusti* prayer, which accompanies the untying and retying of the *Kusti*, or sacred thread. No layman draws near the altar upon which is set the urn with the undying fire. Only the priest, the *mobed*, or the high priest, the *dastur*, may come close to the fire. Even the present-day successor to the Magi wears a cloth over his mouth and nostrils, lest his breath should pollute the flame.

The other indispensable building, the *Dakhma*, is the Tower of Silence, where, according to the ancient Magian practice, the corpses of the dead are exposed to the vultures who generally strip a corpse of every shred of flesh in less than an hour. The object of this practice is to protect the elements of fire, earth and water from pollution. Modern-minded Parsis are urging a change over to cremation. But those who cling to ancient usage and to whom age-old customs are precious, explain the Towers of Silence as part of Zoroastrian purity and cleanliness, and as a means of protecting the living from contagion.

The High Priest of the Parsis in Karachi, Dr. N. M. Dhalla, concludes a noble and scholarly *History of Zoroastrianism* with a very pertinent observation. During the three thousand years, more or less, of Zoroastrianism, great and famous monarchs, kings and emperors, have ruled Iran. Today they are hardly even memories. Who remembers Darius Xerxes, or Artaxerxes? But the personality of Zarathushtra, in whom was centered the spiritual power of their people, still rules in the hearts of a very vivid company of devotees, and will continue to rule for ages to come.

In heartening show of friendship, Zoroastrian priest and Moslem teacher walk in old School of Four Gardens in Ispahan, Iran. Advocating spiritual education for all, the Zoroastrians strongly oppose communism in Persia.

**BEFORE TOWERING TABLETS** bearing Ten Commandments, 30,000 Jews throng New York Garden to witness pageant, "We Will

Never Die," marking 4,000 years of Jewish history.

# 8. JUDAISM

*Hear, O Israel: The Lord
Our God, the Lord Is One*

THE POWERFUL FIGURE IN Michelangelo's statue presents Moses as a superhuman being of tremendous strength, a demiurge, of all but supernatural creative force.

The sculptor has truly grasped the character of the man. For, whereas other Teachers and prophets brought a religion to a people, Moses conceived the stupendous idea of creating a people for a religion. By the force and intensity of his will, he undertook the amazing project of hammering out a nation to carry, to live by, to embody in every phase and act of existence, the idea of one God, the One, eternal, all-powerful, who always is and ever will be. So incisive was the impact of the Mosaic teaching that even today, after 3,500 years, much of the ethics and most of the morals of our world still hark back to it. Both Christianity and Islam are offshoots of the religion he brought to mankind, and all three are still thriving in full vigor.

Who was Moses, that man of towering genius? The origin of the entire Hebrew people is still obscure. They were desert folk drifting about with their flocks much as Bedouins still do today. But at least one of their groups had had contact with an ancient center of Sumero-Accadian civilization, known as Ur—Ur of the Chaldees. The head or sheikh of the group was the patriarch Abraham. He did not stay there long. Some nineteen hundred years before the Christian Era, the empire of Sumer and Accad suddenly collapsed under the onslaught of barbarians—those energetic people who had also invaded Iran and India. Abraham moved on—to the southwest, where grazing was possible.

The Book of Genesis in the Bible begins with allegory, and some have made the mistake of taking it all as allegory. But discovery after discovery of nineteenth- and twentieth-century archeology has tended more and more to render the biblical record acceptable to scholars. And as Professor Salo Baron puts it: "The lifelike description of the human

In Old World, orthodox Israelis say morning prayers. Youths wear skullcaps, shawls and *tefillin* which are wound around arm, each twist signifying a virtue. Tefillin rite is performed daily except on the Sabbath.

strengths and weaknesses of Abraham, Isaac, Jacob and Joseph in the book of Genesis is also more likely to reflect actual historical personalities than mere personifications of later Hebrew tribes."

The "lifelike description" is one of the great secrets of the power and survival of that truly astonishing record known as the Bible. So real do those semi-nomadic patriarchs of perhaps four thousand years ago seem to us today that we can still follow with breathless interest their forward movement into history, the romance of Jacob and his wives and sons, the sale of his beloved Joseph into slavery in Egypt and the coming to Egypt of the very sons, who so cruelly had sold their brother, in search of food in a time of dearth. And could

anything be more dramatic than the episode of their finding that the brother they had sold for a slave was actually the ruler of Egypt, to whom they had come for favors? And not the least of the dramatic factors is that, for all their ancient perfidy, they found not hatred but love in the heart of Joseph.

History points to a conquest of Egypt about 1750 B.C. by Aryan invaders called Hyksos, the "shepherd kings," who encouraged their Semitic allies, and notably the Hebrews. It was a Hyksos Pharaoh who appointed Joseph as "governor," or Prime Minister. But after the Hyksos were expelled, nearly two centuries later, by the original Egyptians, the Hebrews remained in Egypt. Then came to the throne a Pharaoh, perhaps Rameses II, who de-

In New World, reform New Yorkers dedicate new temple at Forest Hills. Ornamental Ark (rear) contains sacred Scrolls of Torah, the first Five Books of Old Testament and most revered object in Hebrew history.

cided to build and rebuild certain cities and vast pyramids. In quest of large forces of labor, he turned toward the Apiru, or Hebrews, living close to his capital, Tanis, in the land of Goshen.

The Bible tells us how oppressed the Hebrews were, how actually enslaved in their compulsion to forced labor. The lash of the overseers whipped them to impossible tasks. "Bricks without straw" has passed into the language as an intolerable condition of labor. We hear of forced labor in parts of the world today, but three and a half millennia ago, before civilization had made much headway, it was still a novelty. The cry of the oppressed laborers was rising constantly. From among them, however, arose an heroic figure, who was later to become known as the most famous of human lawgivers, the man Moses.

The traditional story of his being concealed by his mother in an ark of papyrus reeds, and placed among the rushes beside the bank of the Nile, is too well known to need detailed repetition. How the daughter of the Pharaoh found him and brought him up as her son, unwittingly hiring his own mother as nurse, is graphically told in Genesis and has become one of the great legends of mankind. In any case, though he was educated as a priest of Osiris, learned in all the knowledge of the Egyptians, he turned to his own people, resolved to free them from their bondage.

That agglomeration of Asiatics, mostly Semitic,

were by no means all descendants of Jacob. These latter may have carried memories of the God of Abraham, El Shaddai, for whose sake the patriarch was ready to sacrifice his son, Isaac. To Moses, at any rate, the Egyptian polytheism and animal worship was repulsive. According to Exodus, the one God, Yahveh, whom he worshiped and proclaimed, revealed Himself to Moses while he was herding his father-in-law's flocks in the mountains of Midian. That tremendous religious experience, which has meant so much to countless Jews and Christians alike, is described in the Bible in some very brief paragraphs:

"And the angel of the Lord appeared unto him in a flame of fire out of the midst of a bush: and he looked, and, behold, the bush burned with fire, and the bush was not consumed."

The story of how the Lord instructed Moses to deal with Pharaoh and to deal with the Hebrews, whom He had chosen as his own people, is one of the most fascinating in the Bible. With all the available aid of Egyptian magic, of his brother Aaron's eloquence and, above all, his own genius, Moses succeeded in unifying a people in a unifying God. By sheer spiritual power he imposed upon a more or less heterogeneous collection of Semites his own lofty monotheism. He led them out of Egypt into the desert, gave them a code of ethics and a code of laws and, in short, created a people that has exercised a tremendous influence, has given birth to two other great world religions and, in spite of all persecutions, survives and flourishes to this day.

That human engineering so decisively set in motion by Moses has persisted through more than three thousand years of history and a record of vicissi-

Judaism is one of the two world religions (the other is Sikhism) which neither encourages nor practices pilgrimages. The exception, proving the rule, takes place annually at Meron where 40,000 to 50,000 Israelis gather to honor the memory of the greatest Cabalist, Shimeon Bar-Yochai. This stalwart rabbi, who nearly 2,000 years ago defied the Roman legions from a Galilean mountain hideout and who wrote his masterpiece on occult Cabala, the *Zohar*, while living in a cave, lies buried in Meron. His tomb and that of his son, Rabbi Eleazer, are the goal of the pilgrimage which occurs on *Lag Ba'omer* or 33rd day between Exodus from Egypt and giving of Commandments on Mt. Sinai. Like all Jewish Holy Days, the celebration begins at sundown with carrying of the Torah (above) from Safed to Meron. And, as is the custom, nearly every devout family shaves the heads of its three-year-olds (right), sparing only two traditional side twists and saving the cut curls for years to come.

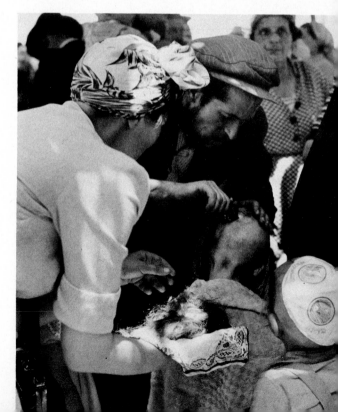

tudes unmatched by any people on earth. The covenant, or contract, between the Lord and his people Moses proclaimed at the foot of Mount Sinai, has held to this day. Its basis was the Ten Commandments, still the basis of Western civilization. The immediate task, that of the conquest of Canaan by the tribes of Israel, began at once and lasted a long time. The taking of Jerusalem, for instance, which was to become the capital, took some two hundred years. But the Israelites never stopped. This was the "promised land," promised by Jehovah himself. They were bound to take it, since by that promise it was already theirs.

But in the way stood many obstacles. The Jebusites, the Edomites, the Moabites, the Ammonites—a whole aggregation of peoples had to be overcome. And the Philistines—how large they loom in Bible history! They came originally from Crete and were powerful and troublesome fighters. Where are they all? Swept down the sluices and channels of history, into oblivion. That is, they would have been wholly forgotten but for their mention in the Bible. It seems hard to imagine how a people can settle a land, practice the arts of peace, and yet be at all times and continuously on a war footing, as must have been the post-Exodus Hebrews. But that is the way the Hebrews lived for centuries. And every now and then we have a reminder that the Israelis of today, after a gap of thirty-odd centuries, are again living that way in the Canaan or Palestine they have reconquered.

The biblical record is graphic with the story of the Hebrews after they burst out of Egypt into history. A rough and earnest lot they were, as they marched into the desert, with the "Ark of the Covenant" carried before them as a symbol of their

Reaching Meron from Safed after dark and signaling start of an all-night jubilee, the pilgrims light candles on tombs of Rabbi Bar-Yochai and touch off bonfires on white-cupolaed roofs (above) which cover the shrine. Ceremonial magic of the Cabala is carried out in secret sessions. Singing, praying, pushing people fill picturesque streets, overflow into cenotaph building, strew burning candles on tombs until flames leap 15 feet into the air. Hundreds write prayers on pieces of paper and toss them into the blaze. Meanwhile, Hebrew hymns are sung, Lag Ba'omer dances rehearsed and scores of fires lighted upon roofs and surrounding hills. The festival mounts its zenith with the stars until dawn finds many a weary celebrant (left) resting and reading Torah on the hillside. Meron is also cherished as burial spot of Rabbi Hillel, who, challenged by Roman scoffer, summarized the Law in Jewish Golden Rule, "What thou wouldst not have others do unto you, do not do unto others."

141

*Yeshivabouchers*, or young pupils, studying Talmud aloud in Tel Aviv school, represent orthodox practice in struggle with secular education. Pious lads, who study 10 hours daily, learn 63 tractates of Talmud. Compendium of law and lore, written by ancient rabbis, is treasure house of wisdom, humor, moral maxims.

faith. The ark presumably contained the Ten Commandments—and little else. They had little, those fugitive nomads, but by that little they set tremendous store. They conquered their Canaan across Jordan and proceeded to cultivate the land, establish their trades and make the promised "milk and honey" flow. Some of their neighbors were idolators and worshiped Baal and even the terrible Carthaginian god, Moloch. There were other cults, too, like the cult of Astarte. And cults are contagious. But somehow Yahveh held. The books of the Pentateuch from Exodus to Deuteronomy are the record, stern and uncompromising, of the laws and prescriptions by which that nation, virtually created by the hands and mind of Moses, was kept in check and rigidly controlled for Yahveh or Jehovah.

The backslidings were numerous. But like so many prodigal sons, they always returned to their Father. "If they had not been particularistic and pugnacious," declares a writer on the Old Testament, "we should never have heard of them or of the Kingdom of God." Particularistic, pugnacious, stiff-necked, as the Bible describes them, they certainly were. Hence the long annals of wars and slaughters and sins and cruelties, which none proclaimed more loudly than themselves. Is it perhaps owing to that loud outcry about their own sins and backslidings that they exist as a people today? Is it owing to their obedience to the original charge to hold themselves as the people of I AM that they have survived the tremendous breakage and dissolution of nations which continues to this day? Their survival is one of the miracles of history. Any Jewish or any Christian divine will tell you that the reason they survived is because of their powerful faith in God.

That unconquerable faith in God, however, was to be kept constantly and ceaselessly alive. In an-

Good Samaritans of 20th century, descendants of first Israelites, chant Old Testament prayers to start Passover Festival on Mount Gerizim in Samaria.

White-robed elders of tribe, which follows Law of Moses, quote from Pentateuch, recall flight of Jews from Egypt, finally order slaying of sacrificial rams.

cient Israel, it was kept alive by a species of men no other nation ever quite matched. We mean the long succession of Hebrew prophets. Through the centuries of "judges" first, then under a series of kings, those men of vision, some of them untutored peasants or herdsmen, like Amos, kept appearing, appointed and called, they declared, of God, appearing and prophesying. Their prophecies dealt at least as much with the past as with the future. For priestly ritualism so prevalent in all Near Eastern religions at that time, they cared not at all. As to blood sacrifices to Jehovah, these were declared to be an abomination rather than a satisfaction to the Lord. As Micah, one of the chain of prophets, said:

> What doth the Lord require of thee?
> Save to do justice, to love mercy,
> And to walk humbly with thy God.

The smugness of routine religion was repeatedly shattered by these men. Israel, they announced, had not a chance of life or survival unless it practiced real religion. As Lewis Browne puts it: "Had it not been for those few prophets, Israel would today be no more than Idumea or Philistia. Had it not been for their insight and courageous labor, Yahveh would have been no more to civilization than Baal-Melkart or Dagon. Sons in blood to Moses, brethren in spirit to Ikhnaton, Zoroaster, Buddha, and Lao-Tse, they loom up in the story of religion as veritable supermen."

Insight and courageous labor was undoubtedly theirs. But they had so much more than that. Vision, clairvoyance, vaticination and inspiration were also theirs. There were actually schools of prophets. Some of the great ones, such as Samuel or Elisha, had their pupils and followers, like artists, or Greek philosophers. At times, they were treated by popu-

Hebraism's holy place—the Wailing Wall of Jerusalem—is as sacred to Jews today as it was nearly 3,000 years ago when it formed part of magnificent Temple of King Solomon. The Temple was begun by Psalmist King David, who, after defeating the Philistines and making Jerusalem the capital of Judah, purchased building site for 50 shekels of silver. Construction proceeded under direction of David's son Solomon, who not only finished the Temple but raised the ancient kingdom to a fabulous peak of power and affluence. Built in seven years and raised to the glory of Jehovah, the Temple endured until 586 B.C. when Jerusalem was sacked by the Babylonians. Through the long centuries, worshiping Jews, like their modern descendants (above and right), came to the crumbling 156-foot Wall to bewail the downfall of Jerusalem and the razing of the first Temple. To this day, when permitted by Arabs during holy festival periods, the faithful gather here to pray and read the Five Books of Moses.

lace and rulers like princes; at other times like nuisances, if not like convicts. Yet the prophets saved Israel and remain to this day a priceless heritage of both the Jewish and the Christian religions.

They were not merely Jehovah's witnesses—all Israelites were that—they were Jehovah's champions. They made and unmade kings, as did the prophet Samuel, or they were hunted fugitives, like Jeremiah. They were not merely "trouble shooters," trouble was their business. "Thus saith the Lord" was their opening formula, and when the people did not stone them, they believed them. Jeremiah actually had the courage to advise his people to surrender to the Babylonians—because they had defeat and captivity coming to them! Yet the same Jeremiah who foretold the captivity and exile also foretold the liberation and return. And to show his confidence in the future, he bought a piece of land in Jerusalem at the very time Nebuchadnezzar was storming the city.

The aim here is not to tell four thousand years of Jewish history, but to give a brief story of the religion of Judaism. As we see, it is a story of evolution. The Jehovah of Moses, though One, was still a vengeful, jealous, terrible God—such as that primitive horde of desert striders then needed. By the time we come to the prophet Isaiah, about 738 B.C., the lofty monotheism of prophetic Judaism is seen at its best. "Behold, God is my salvation; I will trust, and not be afraid; for the Lord Jehovah is my strength and my song; he also is become my salvation. Therefore with joy shall ye draw water out of the wells of salvation." Isaiah is the prophet of faith. High ideals, spiritual rather than earthly power, those are the things he exalts. The Messianic note struck in the book of Isaiah became an integral part of the Jewish faith. It sustained them through wars, tribulations, exiles and captivities. It kept them alive and united. To a degree it is still doing so today.

The early chronology of the Hebrews goes so far back that writers tend to evade exact dates. The latest history now gives the date of Moses as 1300 B.C. and Rameses II as the probable Pharaoh of the Exodus. If so, there were only about three hundred years between the Exodus and King Saul, whose date is given as 1000 B.C. In the Bible, the time appears much longer. During the next forty years or so, coinciding with the reign of David, Israel was at its most powerful, and in the four decades of Solomon's reign (961-922 B.C.) at its most brilliant. Solomon was enormously wealthy, but also enormously extravagant. The Temple built in Jerusalem during his reign was one of his greatest glories. But so heavy was the tax burden he imposed that directly after his death, in 922, a revolt broke out against his son and successor, Rehoboam. The ten Tribes, later to be known as the Lost Tribes, broke off and formed the Northern Kingdom. Israel suffered its first great cleavage. The disruptive period of Israel had begun. The Northern Kingdom abounded in troubles and bloodshed. The infiltration of Phoenician idolatry with Jezebel of Tyre led to the most burning denunciations by the prophet Elijah. In 722, Sargon II, King of Assyria, conquered and deported virtually the entire population to a region "beyond Jordan," some believe as far as the Caspian Sea.

The remnant of the old kingdom of David, Judah, fared little better. It passed under the Assyrian yoke, then under Egyptian, and finally under Babylon, in what is known as the Captivity. By the waters of Babylon, they sat and wept, but not all the time. Actually the captivity served as a kind of renewal of both their faith and their hopes. The men of the exile included the most intelligent of the kingdom of Judah. They collected the written, and particularly the oral, records about the deeds and lives of their forebears, the patriarchs, the kings and leaders, the prophets. Much of the Pentateuch as well as other books of the Bible were edited, sifted and written down during this period. Besides, were they not a Messianic people, a whole nation dedicated to the task of bringing knowledge of the One God to the Gentiles?

While protecting purity of their 4,000-year-old faith, Jews usually took on cultural coloring of lands to which they emigrated. Synagogue architecture accurately reflects this spirit. New York's massive Reform Temple Emanu-El (left), made famous by many preëminent rabbis, reflects modern splendor of Fifth Avenue, while St. Louis' flaring, futuristic B'nai Amoona Temple (right) shows sweep and vision of Middle West. One of greatest European synagogues is Karoly Körut Temple in Budapest, which in its towers, cupolas, ornate mosaics and marble veneering shows Byzantine-Moslem influences of lower Balkans.

Of all world faiths, Judaism most exalts home worship. From the regular observance of Sabbath (left) to ceremonial feast ending Yom Kippur (above), Jewish families pledge themselves to Most High in quiet ceremonies binding both children and adults to religious living. Thanksgiving and gratitude to God characterize this cycle of festivals which are so numerous a 19th-century rabbi once remarked, "The Catechism of the Jew is his calendar." *Rosh Hashanah*, or New Year, which takes place in early fall, ushers in the Days of Awe, a ten-day period of penance and spiritual stock-taking during which devout right themselves with King of the Universe. *Yom Kippur*, or Day of Atonement, when penitential period ends, is for all Jews whether orthodox, conservative or reform a time of fasting, self-purification, charitableness and asking of God's forgiveness of sins. In home and synagogue, all believing Jews dedicate themselves anew to "God, merciful, gracious, long-suffering, abundant in goodness and ever true." Similarly, throughout year, good Jews observe many Holy Days which remind them of glorious events in the past and their dependence upon God in the present. Among most significant festivals are Passover, Purim, Succoth, Simchas Torah, Pesakh, Chanukah and Shavuos.

148

*Chanukah* or Festival of Lights, beloved by children, celebrates Maccabees' victory over Syrians. It is marked by lighting of eight candles of faith, freedom, courage, love, charity, integrity, knowledge and peace.

Sabbath begins Friday at sundown, when mother lights candles and prays, "May our home be consecrated, O God, by thy light." Sacred day for most Jews is time for worship and rest as well as happy home celebrations.

When Cyrus the Persian conquered Babylon in his turn, he restored Israel to its homeland and allowed the Temple to be rebuilt in 516. That made a center for their religious faith and their culture. And though many never came back from their colonies, outposts and places of exile, their veneration of, and attachment to, the Holy City was all the stronger. Under Persian rule, the Hebrew commissioner, Ezra, came armed with royal power to make the Law of Moses as absolutely mandatory as the royal laws of Persia. That Law, the *Torah*, remained mandatory after the conquest by the Greek Alexander the Great, after the conquest and destruction of Jerusalem by the Romans in A.D. 70 and on into the Diaspora in all parts of the world. For the orthodox, it remains mandatory today. They were, and became all the more intensely, the People of the Book.

Thus nineteen centuries ago, their career, of about the same number of centuries gone before, culminated in a dispersal such as no other people had ever experienced. At that time there was as yet no organized Christianity, no Islam, no European nations, no Arab states. There was only imperial Rome, and the seeds of its decay were already germinating. The Jews seemed to be ended with those dead and gone empires of the past, the empires of Babylon and Egypt, of Sargon and Darius, Artaxerxes and Alexander the Great. But, as they moved out into new and strange regions, they carried their Book. In the desert out of Egypt they had borne the Ark of the Covenant with the Ten Commandments. Now they had not even an Ark. The Book alone was shield and buckler, palladium and pillar of fire. To Spain and Portugal, to Italy, Greece and The Levant, to France, Holland, Germany, Poland and Austria and the Russian steppes, everywhere, they brought the Book. Of course, they had more than the one book. They had the Talmud and the Mishna, texts like Maimonides' *Guide to the Perplexed*, the Cabala, the Zohar, a rich and intricate literature, both religious and secular. But the foundation of all was the Book— the Bible.

To medieval Europe, most of whose inhabitants could neither read nor write, that was something of a red rag. With the coming of the Crusades in the eleventh century, when all Christendom was arrayed against the Moslem possessor of the Holy Sepulcher, the word "infidel" became a terrible incitement to violence. The European mobs forgot that the peaceful Jews among them held no Holy Sepulcher, or anything else. With the German spirit that revealed itself anew in Hitler's time, a

For every Jewish boy, the most important day of his life is *Bar Mitzvah*—the day he becomes a man or "Son of the Law." The confirmation ceremony, which takes place when a boy is 13 and which occurs in synagogue, is conducted by the rabbi in presence of parents, relatives and friends. Preparing for event itself and religious responsibilities of manhood, Jewish lad studies Torah for years, learns Hebrew, memorizes ancient hymns and prayers. During confirmation, he wears such articles of faith as the *tallith* or shawl and *tefillin* or arm bands, symbol of his right to worship with adults. Rabbi, relatives and adult friends take turns reciting Scripture in Hebrew and English. Standing before Sacred Ark, rabbi removes the Torah, hands it to boy's father who in turn passes it to his son, thus, symbolizing continuity of the Law. Young candidate, then, reads from Torah and Book of Psalms, leads congregation in prayer and, finally, is confirmed as a man by rabbi (above). Solemn ceremony of dedication recalls to young and old alike heroic heritage of Jewish people.

Among gifts received by Bar Mitzvah are morning prayer book and leather phylacteries. Headpiece and arm **bands** signify surrender of head and heart to God's will.

→

Wearing orthodox prayer shawl and skullcap, 13-year-old Carl Bodek of Philadelphia strains to open 400-year-old Torah during Bar Mitzvah. Rabbi David Novoseller charged Carl to be true, for "Truth is seal of God."

→

Touro Synagogue in Newport, R. I., is oldest Jewish temple in U.S. With a congregation dating back to 1658 and a temple dedicated in 1763, Rhode Island Jews are proud of national shrine. Rabbi, cantors and trustees observe Sabbath wearing Spanish prayer shawls and using prayer books 200 years old.

frightful slaughter of the Jews began in Germany and spread to other countries. The persecutions then started continued for centuries, with ghetto segregation, badges of shame and expulsions from one country after another. In their expulsion from Spain, in 1492, a dramatic writer represented them as intoning the words of the crucified Jesus: *Eli Eli, lama sabachthani?* My God, my God, why hast thou forsaken me? No answer was forthcoming. But that did not lead them to rebellion. Their faith and their Law they would not part with, come what might.

They studied their Law, saw to it that their children learned the Bible and the Talmud, and kept their festival and fast days without interruption. Passover or *Pesakh,* the anniversary of their flight from Egypt under Moses; *Shavuos,* or Pentecost; *Rosh Hashanah,* or New Year's Day, the Day of Atonement or *Yom Kippur,* and a number of lesser holidays, like the Feast of Tabernacles, the Feast of Lights, the Feast of *Purim,* commemorating Esther's intervention on their behalf in Persia—these are the more important of their holidays. Through the centuries, ever since the destruction of the Temple, they have solemnly wished each other long life, with the added rider: "Next year in Jerusalem." Messianism, the belief in a coming Messiah, never left them. They have had many disappointments. False Messiahs would turn up from time to time, as, for instance, Sabbatai Zevi in the seventeenth century, who wound up as a doorkeeper in the Sultan's palace at Constantinople. But hope and faith were their chiefest possessions.

They have had their long chain of rabbis, scholars, even what might be called mahatmas. One such was famous among them as Israel Bal Shem, that is, the Master of the Name. The tradition was that he who could speak the Lord's name correctly could perform any wonders he desired. And, indeed, this man was something of a wonder-worker and faith healer. He scorned narrow learning and the ceaseless poring over Talmudic texts. It left no time, he said, to think of God, who is everywhere and all about. It pleased God more, he maintained, when he enjoyed his pipe than if he were to sit brooding over the meaning of an obscure Hebrew word. His followers were called *Hasidim,* "the pious ones," and in Poland they were still in existence in the twentieth century. They danced in ecstasy when they prayed and observed minutely every pious facet of their faith.

With the release of the Jews from the ghettos after Napoleon, and especially by the revolutionary wars of 1848, a more liberal view of the rigid Mosaic

Russian Jews crowd a Moscow temple to observe Rosh Hashanah. Although religion is not encouraged in the Soviet, believers are free to frequent open churches.

←

and other ritualistic prescriptions naturally followed. Reform Judaism today, outwardly at least, resembles some of the Protestant Christian sects. In America, it is widely prevalent. The vast majority of Jews throughout the world, however, remain orthodox. For them their religion is not merely an affair of Sabbath keeping and holiday worship, but a way of life, a framework that encloses existence from the cradle to the grave, during every hour and moment of time. It is not only that they still expect the Messiah to come and redeem them, not merely prayers several times a day, but every act, every movement, virtually every thought, takes place with reference to the Deity to whom their lives are dedicated. Judaism does not believe in monasticism. But Brother Lawrence, the French monk, noted for his practice of the presence of God, was no more concentrated in his ceaseless worship than is the thoroughly orthodox Jew.

And since the greatest concentration of members of the Jewish faith is in the United States (about 5,200,000 on the North American continent) it may be of interest to see how that ancient faith is practiced in America today. Mr. Frank S. Mead in his *Handbook* lists these four divisions of Judaism: Orthodox Judaism, "by far the largest body in the United States," Reform Judaism, Conservative Judaism and Reconstruction Judaism. The three older organizations are all members of the Synagogue Council of America. Reconstruction Judaism is a new movement. It was established only in 1940 and its aim is the creation of a world-wide cooperative Jewish Society. Its membership thus far is not large. But whatever the division, it can hardly be called a denomination. For all divisions are bound together by their millennial faith and profession of unity, and the oneness of God: "Hear, O Israel, the Lord is our God, the Lord is One." Every Jew who practices his religion at all repeats this declaration daily. It is the self-same prayer in modern America, as was heard in ancient Judea.

The largest of the branches, or divisions, is certainly the Orthodox. The Bible, that is the Torah, the Prophets and the Writings, as well as the Talmud, the Mishna and their commentaries, make up the backbone of authority for the Orthodox. It is all they carried away from their tribulations and persecutions in the Old World and transplanted under the free sun of the New. Even as did their predecessors two thousand years ago, they still hope for and await the Messiah, still observe, many of them, the dietary laws laid down in the Pentateuch, and pray for the rebuilding of the temple in Jerusalem. On their great festivals, like *Rosh Hashanah*

In synagogue courtyard in Warsaw, Rabbi Uziel conducts Torah class for teen-age Poles. Nearly 6,000,000 Jews died in Europe during Hitlerian reign of terror.

➤

Black Jews of Harlem, who today number nearly 5,000, form part of world-wide Jewish community. Rabbi W. A. Matthews (above), founder of Commandment Keepers Congregation, preaches sermon at Saturday services. Negro Jews maintain synagogues in Chicago, Philadelphia, Cincinnati, Africa, West Indies and Europe.

Great *Diaspora* or dispersion, following Roman destruction of Holy Temple in A.D. 70, made Judaism world-wide religion. Today, with majority of their 12 millions living in Europe and U.S., Jews are scattered from Spain to India, China to Brazil. Reform rabbi (above) leads Indian congregation in Mexico City.

Black Jews of South Africa hold open air service near Johannesburg. Led by spear-wielding Marubo, founder of Apostolic Church of Zion, tribe observes Jewish forms with overtones of Islam and native Zulu. Singing and dancing form lively part of ritual. Congregation wears white robes decorated with Star of David.

Catholic converts to Judaism, who emigrated to Israel from Italy, read prayers in makeshift synagogue in Alma. Eliezer Trito (center) leads service in Italian.

These 80 peasants, who settled in Galilee, were converted in 1940's by reading Old Testament. They are now farming and building homes in Promised Land.

Descendants of Jews, who fled Jerusalem when Titus of Rome sacked the Holy City, maintain their 1,900-year-old community on island of Djerba off Tunisia.

Numbering 5,000 orthodox believers, Djerbas preserve Mosaic purity in religion and living habits. But on entering Ghriba Temple, they remove shoes like Moslems.

*Kubbet Es-Sakhra*, or Sacred Rock, occupies a glorious place in religious legends of both Jews and Moslems. Located near center of Old Jerusalem and measuring 58 by 44 feet, the Rock is venerated by Jews as spot where Lord tested first Hebrew Leader Abraham by commanding sacrifice of his son, Isaac. Even as Abraham, keeper of Covenant with God, sadly obeyed, the Lord released him from the command and allowed him to substitute a ram. To this day, obedience to God's law has remained the foremost tenet of Judaism and imitation of His virtues the center of Jewish morality. Believing themselves both a chosen and a choosing people, Jews have preserved their ethical monotheism for 3,500 years by encouraging love of learning, practicing good deeds, worshiping the one just, timeless, omnipresent, incorporeal Jehovah. And to worship God is to love His creation—Man—for "he that loves his neighbors has fulfilled the Law."

Looming large in bleak expanse of southern Israel, as in the mind of Western man, stand storied peaks of Mt. Sinai (above). Here, amid thunder and lightning 3,500 years ago, God revealed Ten Commandments to Moses and bequeathed a moral legacy to Jewish people which endures to this day. Leader, lawgiver, messenger of the one eternal Jehovah, Moses had prayed for 40 days on the mountain before a Voice spoke to him out of the whirlwind: "I am the Lord thy God, which have brought thee out of the land of Egypt, out of the house of bondage," and then proclaimed to him the Decalogue which makes Judaism an ethical faith of the highest order. The Laws this mighty nation-maker transmitted to his people deepened their belief in one God, fostered virtues of reverence, honor, justice, charity and holiness, profoundly influenced character of Christian and Islamic faiths that followed. Today, Greek Orthodox monastery of St. Catherine occupies the site.

157

and *Yom Kippur,* they still press each other's hands and say, "Next year in Jerusalem."

Reform Judaism, on the other hand, is a broad, liberal interpretation of the faith, reminiscent of the more liberal forms of Christianity. The Reform Jew looks upon such features as the dietary laws, the coming of the Messiah as ancient tenets outgrown by the swift pace and changed conditions of modern life. As to return to Palestine and Jerusalem, that is one solution for Jewish refugees from Europe and displaced persons, but the Reform Jew of today is too solidly based as a citizen in the country that is his present home to seek emigration to a slender strip of desert country. He does, however, sympathize warmly with those to whom it is a necessity. He is, as a rule, patriotic, educated, socially conscious. He is broadly and deeply charitable. In recent years, for instance, American Judaism raises from $150,000,000 to $250,000,000 annually for charity.

Those leaders, the United Jewish Appeal, the Joint Distribution Committee, and the American Jewish Committee, which respectively collect and distribute funds, and protect the religious and civil rights of all Jews on a global scale, are in a sort models of what completely unselfish organizations devoted to charity and justice can do. The division of Conservative Judaism, which of course participates in all these enterprises, steers a middle course between the Orthodox and Reform branches. It is more like the Reform congregation in outward appearance, but like the Orthodox in observation of dietary laws and clinging closely to Zionism and to the Torah. It has had a rapid growth since its founding in the mid nineteenth century, and now has its own seminary in New York. Besides these, there are other small bodies, like Reconstructionism and the Commandment Keepers, a Harlem Negro community which follows Orthodox Judaism. Negro Jews also have congregations in many U.S. and European cities.

Today, in the land of Israel, Judaism has reestablished, in a manner that has astonished the world, its ancient home and habitation. From the four corners of the earth its devotees strain to return there. By tens of thousands they arrive there every year. But shadings and gradations of creed seem inescapable. For here, too, in the very cradle of their faith, the struggle still continues between the liberal and modernized and their orthodox co-religionists, who would return to, or practice, the religion of the Temple era, and all the ancient pieties.

Jerusalem the Golden, now 3,000 years old and scarred by invasions of Assyrians, Persians, Egyptians, Greeks, Romans and Arabs, dreams on its hilltop in the new Israel. Sacred to Jews since King David unified the 12 Wandering Tribes and brought Ark of the Covenant to the walled city, Jerusalem has looked the same for

centuries. Today, although venerated by Christians as the Holy City and by Arabs as the Holy, *Yerushalayim* or City of Peace is still the spiritual heart of Hebrew race and religion. The panorama (above) shows at left the lower slope of Mount of Olives and at right of many-domed church in center is Garden of Gethsemane. In right background stands dark-domed Mosque of Omar, believed by Jews to be site of Temple of Solomon and revered by Moslems as spot where Prophet Mohammed flew directly to heaven. To Jew, Gentile, Arab alike, the ancient city yet proclaims, "The Earth is the Lord's and the fullness thereof."

# 9. CHRISTIANITY

*Thou shalt love the Lord thy God with all thy heart and soul, and thou shalt love thy neighbor as thyself*

NO RELIGION, IT HAS BEEN SAID, has expressed higher ideals than those of Christianity, and none has been farther from achieving them. Who has not heard the glib remark that Christianity is a wonderful religion but that it has not yet been tried? Nevertheless, it remains true that we owe to Christianity and its parent religion of Judaism, the very basis of our ethics, all that we know of compassion, charity, kindness, mercy, forbearance and the love of God.

Imagine for a moment what our European-American civilization might have been had we inherited one of the pre-Christian cults that contained the adulterous Greek gods, or the gloomy pantheon of ancient Rome, or the brawling divinities of Valhalla! It does not bear thinking about. The story of the coming of Christianity is perhaps the most stirring and appealing in the annals of mankind, and to this day, after two thousand years, it remains new.

The Mediterranean world at about the beginning of our era had marked resemblances to the present time. For one thing, it was filled with fear and hatred. The powerful empire of Rome consisted largely of subjugated lands and peoples, none of whom bore any love for their conquerors. To the conquered, imperial Rome appeared as a cold, materialistic, ruthless power, virtually without religion, possessing only policies. One of

Jesus of Nazareth, who became the Christ and who died on Cross for sinning mankind, established religion of love which today has 600 million followers in every nation of world.

her policies was indeed peace, but it was Roman peace—secured by the sword. A number of her emperors, such as Tiberius, Caligula, Nero, were then held and are still remembered as horrible examples of depravity. They were the ones who ruled all the then known world.

Among the many conquests made by irresistible Rome, the latest was a small, stubborn, unreconciled, fiercely religious people of Asia Minor, known as the Jews. To these, with their long history of religion, austerity and devotion, the cold materialistic, calculating Romans were like a breed from another planet. It was not a case of imperfect sympathy. There was no sympathy at all. Both peoples were detestable to each other. The Romans preferred conquests like those of Greece or Egypt. They could be held in leash. If you gave them a statue of a Tiberius and ordered them to worship it, or to "Heil Caesar," heil Caesar they did. With the Jews, it was different. They refused. They could not worship human beings. Why not? Their Law forbade it. They could worship only the one God, of whom no statue could ever be made. The Roman governors themselves may have had no love for Tiberius, but they were there to see that Rome was obeyed. They had legions of very well-drilled troops to prove it. In consequence, there were always incidents, abortive insurrections, bloodshed, cruelty, hatred and death.

Into this world, behind

Church Eternal and Holy Bible represent substance and spirit of every Christian's faith. Church as mystical body of Christ and Bible as revealed Word of God offer man divine guidance during his pilgrimage on earth.

the spear-point curtain, in the family of a simple Jewish carpenter of Nazareth in Palestine, was born the child Jesus, later called the Messiah or Christ, perhaps the most beloved human being ever born on earth.

Every birth is the beginning of a drama. With the birth of Jesus opened not only the greatest of religious dramas, but the most moving of all human dramas known to our race. It is a drama for which even today, after two thousand years, most of the inhabitants throughout three continents, and many in the rest of the world, could act as prompters.

That legend and symbol in rich abundance cluster about the narrative of that unique life goes without saying. And every legend, be it remembered, has its base of truth. Not without meaning is the birth of Jesus pictured in a stable. God-like man is not often an inhabitant of earthly palaces, and even in the lowliest places may appear divine love.

The rulers of Palestine were, of course, the Romans. But Rome had a way of keeping and using local "stooge" kings, much as satellite countries today are ruled under Russian communism by local Communists. The sons of Herod ruled various sections of Palestine; Judea, Samaria and Idumea were ruled by Archelaus, a brutal tyrant, too brutal even for Rome. Augustus Caesar duly deposed him and put in his place a procurator, or governor, sent direct from Rome. Pontius Pilate was one of those procurators. The home of Jesus was in Galilee, ruled by Herod Antipas, one of the sons. This was a quieter section as well as a more cosmopolitan one. There were almost as many foreigners, Greeks, Phoenicians, Syrians, as there were Jews. Herod Antipas laid himself out to Romanize and Hellenize the region, building cities, forums, baths, colonnades, with taxes increasing almost daily. Certain among the Jews, never in love with Rome, found this to be intolerable and proceeded to organize the rebel party known as the Zealots. They actually did try rebellion and took the city of Sepphoris. Rome sent up a couple of legions, and literally thousands of the Zealots were crucified in stamping out the revolt.

Most of the Jews, however, had no connection with violence, awaited the coming of the Anointed One, the Messiah, who would free them from all tribulations, and followed a policy of pray and bear it. Some, like the Pharisees and Sadducees, were steeped in learning and ritual. Others were devout, God-fearing and industrious, without any great learning. It is of these that Jesus was born.

Though we think of him as born in the year A.D.

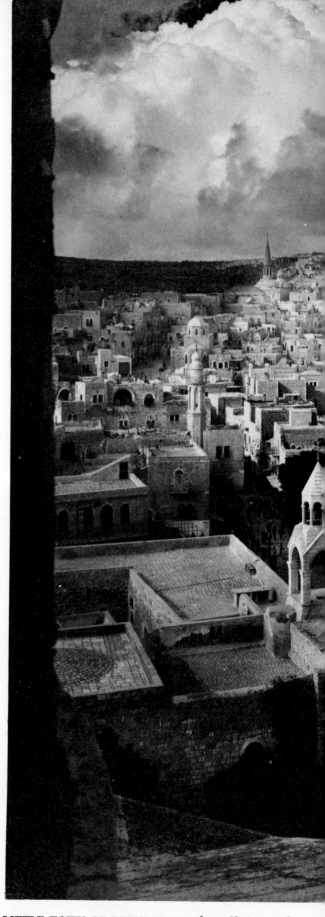

**LITTLE TOWN OF BETHLEHEM,** where Christ was born,

etches away toward hills of Judea. Today its 75,000 population is composed of Catholic, Greek Orthodox, Armenian, Coptic Christians.

1, he was actually born about 4 B.C. Some say 6 B.C. The error arose some centuries later in the reckoning of the monks, when time began to be dated from the birth of Christ. His father Joseph was, as we know, a carpenter, and his brothers and sisters were numerous. Familiar is the story of Joseph and Mary on their travels: How, at Bethlehem, Mary was overtaken by illness, and there was no room at the inn. In the manger, however, her only shelter for the night, her Child was born, and, according to the legend, shepherds no less than Wise Men, or kings, brought their gifts and offerings to this Babe who was to remake the world. Those symbols of love and adoration are posterity's constant reminder that no honor and no devotion are too great for a God-like man.

Of his childhood so little is known that one marvels at our lack of knowledge of even the greatest lives. One episode is so constantly stressed that it must be true. While traveling with his father and mother, Jesus as a child of twelve was suddenly lost. We can understand the anguish of his mother until she found him after a heartbreaking search, in the temple. How is it, he asked . . .

"How is it that ye sought me? Wist ye not that I must be about my Father's business?"

Not his earthly father's. Already his consciousness was so permeated by the tie between him and his Father in Heaven, he was astonished that his elders should ignore it. Why, the child seemed to say, that is our supreme occupation on earth. You, so much older than I, must surely know that. Yes, in a way they knew it. In a way we all know it. But that child of twelve was already living it. His Father—the Father of all mankind—making all humanity brothers and sisters, one family! If the drama were not all so tremendous, this would strike us with explosive force. "It is written," Jesus later said, "that man shall not live by bread alone, but by every word of God." Physical food becomes a starvation diet in view of such vitalizing, electrifying knowledge as he carried within him even as a child of twelve.

Yet, for eighteen years after that episode, we hear nothing whatever of Jesus. The conjectures about those silent years are numerous. Hindus, for example, believe that Jesus visited India during this time and learned much about Indian wisdom. The Irish novelist, George Moore, in *Brook Kerith*

Church of Nativity, built by Constantine in A.D. 330 over grotto where Jesus was born, is oldest Christian church. On Christmas Eve, crowds and choir, guarded by Arab Legion, fill Manger Square for midnight mass.

2,000 Christian pilgrims crowd Church of Nativity (left) for Christmas services which begin when Alberto Gori, Catholic Patriarch of Jerusalem, enters church carrying "infant" Jesus. Greek Orthodox observance (below) is held week later with same pomp and pageantry.

In Jerusalem, the Garden of Gethsemane, where Jesus was betrayed by Judas and resolved to be martyred, still blooms at foot of Mount of Olives. On site where Son of Man and disciples prayed to "Our Father who art in heaven," there now stands Catholic Church of all Nations and cupolaed Russian Orthodox Cathedral.

In California, Yosemite National Park cradles Protestant sunrise service. 2,000 years and 5,000 miles removed from Christianity's storied beginnings, United States represents its latest and greatest pinnacle of power. With 55 million Protestants and 31 million Catholics, U.S. Christianity is world force for good.

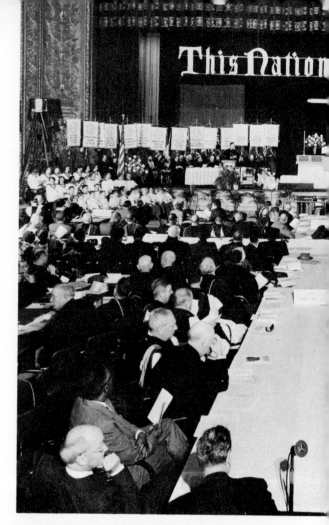

"Go ye into all the world, and preach," Jesus told Twelve Disciples by shores of Galilee. Franciscan monk looks across low-lying Sea where Christ walked on water and multiplied loaves and fishes. From obscure corner of Roman Empire, Christianity spread into 70 countries.

Good news of Gospel, brought to America by Pilgrims and pioneers 300 years ago, has produced astounding array of 251 Christian sects, 285,277 local churches, and total membership of 88 millions. Steady growth of various religious groups has made U.S. the largest Prot-

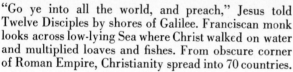

paints an elaborate picture of Jesus as a shepherd in the hills for the Essene community at Engaddi. The Essenes were a monastic order, also called the therapeuts, devoted to religion and healing. But if Jesus was an Essene, why do the Gospels never mention it? Disciples were bound by an unbreakable oath of silence.

Possible though these things are, the more probable is that Joseph, who disappears from the story during this interval, died, and Jesus, assisted by his brothers, took over the carpenter shop and plied his trade for the good of the family.

In the Graeco-Roman world, at about that time, people seemed to be waiting for something to happen, some great cosmic event, some mighty and compelling spiritual revolution. Many were awaiting a redeemer, a Messiah, but none hoped and prayed for him more fervently than did the Jews. During so many centuries of wars and captivities

and dispersions, they had somehow escaped extinction. They held themselves as the people of the One God, and the certainty of the coming of a Messiah to reunify them in their unity, to unify the world so that the lion and the lamb might lie down together, had become their most cherished tradition.

Many an itinerant preacher, anchorite and self-styled prophet was going about Judea and other parts of Palestine during those first years of our era. With varying degrees of fervor and conviction those holy men were proclaiming that the time was at hand, the day was fast approaching, the Messiah was not far off and must soon appear.

One in particular, Johanan, or John, known as the Baptizer, a man of prophetic stature, was so compellingly earnest, he drew many people to the spot on the banks of the Jordan where he preached. His teaching was characterized by a symbolic ceremony of immersion in the river, as a cleansing and

estant nation in world. Organization of National Council of Churches of Christ (above) in Cleveland in 1950 underscored that growth as well as signaled trend toward Protestant unity. New Council now comprises 30 Protestant denominations and 36 million members.

Christianity's Living Word went around earth, even unto islands of Pacific. Dogura schoolboys, gathered around Station Cross in Papua, New Guinea, are members of tribe Christianized by Methodist missionaries. Today, Christian missions, schools, hospitals dot every land.

a purifying, while awaiting the imminent Messiah. Large numbers accepted his baptism. "Repent," he kept crying out, "for the Kingdom of Heaven is at hand."

And now reappears Jesus of Nazareth, a young man of thirty, whom we had last seen as a child of twelve discussing the Law with the Elders of the synagogue. So deeply stirred was he by the words of John when he came to the encampment on the banks of the Jordan, he, too, accepted baptism at the hands of the Baptist. The Gospel of St. Mark is sternly graphic as to precisely what happened to Jesus as a result of that baptism.

"And straightway coming up out of the water, he saw the heavens opened, and the Spirit like a dove descending upon him:

"And there came a voice from heaven, saying, Thou art my beloved Son, in whom I am well pleased.

"And straightway the spirit driveth him into the wilderness."

At any rate, whatever the religious experience was, it came upon Jesus with tremendous impact. The wilderness was the only possible environment for sorting out his emotions and thinking the matter through. The period of solitude is said to have lasted forty days. At the end of it he decided that the world had nothing to offer compared with the mission so forcefully assigned to him. His mission was to go to the people—not have the people come to him as John the Baptist had done—and proclaim the good news, the "good spell," the Gospel that the reign of God is near, that the Kingdom of Heaven is within us, in every man's heart. And how does one enter that Kingdom, close though it be, closer than breathing, nearer than hands and feet? The first step to it is love. Love is the way to it, the gate, the key, and also the passport.

In shadow of St. Peter's vast and ancient dome, 300,000 Catholics cheer Pope Pius XII with cries of "Viva il Papa," as he opens Church's 24th Holy Year in Rome.

Cathedral, decorated by Raphael and Michelangelo, is largest in Christendom. Present church, which was dedicated by Urban VIII in 1626, dominates the Vatican.

With Pope Pius XII at high altar and with sunlight streaming through lofty windows in cupola, Papal Mass is celebrated in St. Peter's. Beneath bronze altar rest remains of former Popes and of Apostle Peter. Black and gold columns were designed by Bernini. Nearly 100,000 people can worship in six-acre church at once.

It was as simple as that. In every known great teaching, love is a dominant factor, explicitly or implicitly. Love inevitably follows the realization of our identity with the source of all being, our Father. But Jesus alone made love the keystone of his entire structure. He took no chances on any possible error in deduction or reasoning. Love even your enemy, he charged, however difficult that may appear, for that way alone lies safety, health or wholeness, and peace of mind.

He recrossed the Jordan into Galilee and began preaching his good news to the simple people he knew and loved, who in turn were spellbound by his message. Such was the conviction he brought by his divine sincerity and authority that four of his future disciples, Peter, Andrew, James and John, fishermen all, dropped their nets and followed him. The shores of the Lake of Galilee were a sufficient immediate field. What mattered the place if every place in the world was equally in need of the

Twice a year, Greek Orthodox devout headed by King and Queen of Greece make pilgrimage to "miracle island" of Tinos in Aegean Sea. Imploring aid for dying wife, husband (above) prays to Blessed Virgin. Mother (below) carries sick child to Archbishop for blessing.

message? Tiberias, Chorazin, Bethsaida, Capernaum, these were theater enough for the immediate present. All had synagogues and if these were overcrowded by eager listeners, he spoke in the market place, in the field, on the shores of the lake.

He did not care to mingle with scribes or Pharisees. Those gentlemen were too learned and too full of subtleties and doubts. A man without guile pleased him to the point of exclamation, and he was always telling them to become as little children. Little children have virtually no earthly past, and faith and love are natural to them as breathing. Suddenly, possibly to his own surprise as well as to the wonder of the people, he developed the power of healing. He cast out, as they said, the evil spirits. He seemed particularly successful with those mental cases. But just as easily he cured Simon Peter's mother-in-law of a fever and a leper of his leprosy. Crowds now began to follow in his wake.

Sometimes when he preached by the shores of

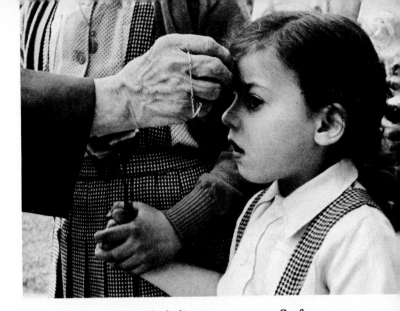

Every Sunday, pious Catholics converge on Carfin, "the Lourdes of Scotland." Here, in Grotto of Our Lady, aged and ailing pray for deliverance. Scotch lass (above) is blessed by relic of St. Thérèse of Lisieux. Priests and nuns (below) pass in town on way to sanctuary.

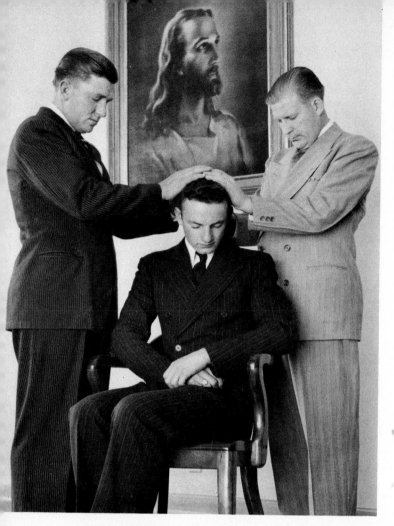

Protestantism in America takes many forms in faith and worship. Yet, beneath surface differences of ordination of Mormon minister, Hyrum Smith, by laying on of hands and erection of roadside Cross by Kentucky Baptist Harrison Mayes, there is basic belief in Fatherhood of God, brotherhood of man, divinity of Jesus.

the lake, the crowd was so dense, he was obliged to enter one of the fishermen's boats and row out a little way so as to leave a strip of water between him and his audience, lest they should crush him. And he spoke to them from the boat. The fourth chapter of Mark gives a vivid picture of his method of teaching. All religious Teachers use fables and parables, but Jesus seemed to be a master in their use. Such a parable as that of the sower scattering his seed, some of it falling to the fowls of the air, some on stony ground and some among thorns, and only a portion falling on good ground, made an indelible impression on those simple minds to whom the picture of the sower was very familiar. Equally clear to them was the figure of the mustard seed, smallest of the seeds, which when grown to full height "shooteth out great branches so that the fowls of the air may lodge under the shadow of it." Then there were the miracles—the loaves and the fishes—the stilling of the waves, the unclean spirits and the swine at Gadara, the revival of the dead child, the daughter of Jairus. Nothing now could keep the throngs of followers from him.

To the plain people, his teaching was more alluring than any they had ever heard. It was not merely that he preached faith in God. All Jews believed in God. It was his *intimacy* with God, his absolutely perfect faith not only in the righteousness of God, but in His mercy, His compassion, His forgiving nature, His utter goodness, His paternal solicitude. He was the Father. All the Father wanted of man is that he make himself fit to enter the Kingdom of Heaven. To do that, man must become perfect as his Father in Heaven is perfect. To do that was man's chief business on earth.

If ever a man was completely identified with God, Jesus of Nazareth was that man. What the Orientals call an avatar, an incarnation of God in a human form, was absolutely exemplified by Jesus. God had sent him to men, not to the Jews alone, but to all men. Almost overnight this thirty-year-old carpenter from Nazareth evinced a power, an authority that could be associated only with the prophets of old, and seemed scarcely of this earth. In the brief space of three years he changed a world. The center of his philosophy, of all his teaching, was love. You must love the Lord your God with all your heart, all your soul and all your mind, and you must love your neighbor as yourself. These two commandments, he said, sum up the whole of the Law and the Prophets. They also sum up all of his teaching. It was not theology he taught, but practical psychology. He disliked fanatic adhesion to the letter

U.S. Protestantism, stressing priesthood of all believers and believer's direct communion with God, is multiplied in thousands of rural parishes across nation. The Rev. Winfield Johnson, pastor of Lutheran Church, Franklin, Minn., stands before congregation and church.

→

Baptism, given different interpretations by different sects, is deemed necessary sacrament by all except Quakers. Archbishop of Detroit, Edward Cardinal Mooney, performs baptismal rite to absolve babies of original sin and restore them to grace. In Presbyterian christening, performed by Rev. Roy E. Howes by sprinkling of water, emphasis is upon invoking of God's blessing and rededication of parents to Christian life.

of the Law. The spirit to him was everything, for man is primarily a spiritual being.

The Samaritans, though also Jews, were regarded as an unclean and a backward people by the rest of Jewry. Jesus, however, who was far too inclusive to harbor such prejudices, one day asked a woman who came to draw water at Jacob's well, for a drink—much to her surprise. The Samaritan woman spoke of her people's worship in the nearby mountains instead of at Jerusalem.

Woman, believe me, Jesus told her, the hour is coming when men will no longer worship either on that mountain or in Jerusalem. But "true worshippers shall worship the Father in spirit and in truth." On that day, exclaims one of his biographers, Jesus was truly the Son of God. He proclaimed the religion for all the world, for all the universe. As to the way of approach to the spirit and the truth, his teaching was brief as it was tremendous. There were the parables, there were a few Beatitudes and the three chapters of the Sermon on the Mount. These make up the sum of his teaching. Probably no single word of it was ever written down by him. The Gospels were written decades later, and at least one of them almost a century after his passing.

In the Gospel of St. Matthew it is said that Jesus "went up into a mountain, and when he was set, his disciples came unto him." There he uttered the Sermon and the Beatitudes. Everyone familiar with the Gospels knows by heart those nine Beatitudes, and many remain bewildered by them. Ages of renderings from Aramaic into Greek, from Greek into Latin and other tongues, have overlaid the meaning with layers of strange coloring, as for instance, "Blessed are the meek, for they shall inherit the earth." Meekness in our time has certain connotations. It makes us think of Uriah Heep and hypocrisy. But the original root of the word meant "gentle." If we say, "Blessed are the gentle," much of our perplexity is at once resolved.

Similarly, "Blessed are the poor in spirit: for theirs is the kingdom of Heaven" could be translated, "Get rid of the hard ego in you, then you can lead the spiritual life." Other Beatitudes are equally brief: "Blessed are they that mourn: for they shall be comforted."

"Blessed are they which do hunger and thirst after righteousness: for they shall be filled."

"Blessed are the merciful: for they shall obtain mercy."

"Blessed are the pure in heart: for they shall see God."

"Blessed are the peacemakers: for they shall be called the children of God."

Some of these are not comprehensible to most of us. "Blessed are the pure in heart, for they shall see God" can have meaning only for the saint, the mystic and the disciples of these. In the words of one commentator, however: "This sentence alone would save mankind, if all books and prophets were lost. This purity of heart will bring the vision of God." But, in general, the precepts are simple. The rest of the Sermon on the Mount is equally simple. Yet it is perhaps the greatest charge to the spiritual life ever given to man. It is the ideal presented here that is so high, man has not yet been able to reach it. For instance:

"Ye have heard that it was said by them of old time, thou shalt not kill; . . .

"But I say unto you, That whosoever is angry with his brother without a cause shall be in danger of the judgment." The vast majority of us have not attained to that point, though in India they will tell you that some of their mahatmas have.

"Agree with thine adversary quickly, while thou art in the way with him." That is, don't let your grudge grow into a feud. A good modern psychiatrist would give the same advice. As Carl Jung, the noted psychotherapist of Zürich wrote: "All religions are therapies for the sorrows and disorders of the soul."

That is what Jesus meant by the words, "the kingdom of Heaven is within you." Thoughts are not merely things. They are the living, the ceaseless molders of our health and our lives. But that we have yet to learn. We can repeat parrotlike over and over, "As a man thinketh in his heart so is he." But we do not believe that applies to us. And who among us takes literally such commandments as: "And if thy right eye offend thee, pluck it out and cast it from thee"? or "if thy right hand offend thee, cut it off and cast it from thee"?

We read these as charges to retain and restore our inner integrity at any cost. Not for Jesus the Old Testament Law, an eye for an eye, and a tooth for a tooth. For him the precept was, resist not evil: "but whosoever shall smite thee on thy right cheek, turn to him the other also." If a man takes away your coat, give him your overcoat as well.

The "resist not evil" principle has caused as much controversy as any single injunction in the Bible. Impossible, we say, to put it into practice. Count Leo Tolstoy was called a madman when he attempted it. Yet in our own time Mahatma Gandhi won great victories by means of the principle of non-resistance. But there are not many Gandhis in the world. All great Teachers, however, have tried to impart that secret to mankind. As one writer puts it: "As soon as you resist mentally any undesirable or unwanted circumstance, you thereby endow it with more power—power which it will use against you, and you will have depleted your own resources to that extent." To hate an evil person is to become that person, more or less. Hatred is a tie that binds us to the object of our hatred, precisely as love links us to the object of our love. Modern psychiatrists are slowly discovering these things.

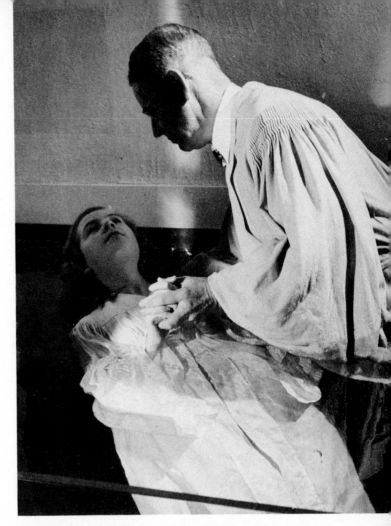

Baptists, who regard baptism as a public confession of faith and symbol of resurrection of Christ, practice immersion because it was mode of baptism used by John the Baptist. At Atlanta's Druid Hills Baptist Church, Rev. Louie Newton (above) baptizes Merle Skinner.

Evangelistic Church of God, which has many branches and half a million members in the U.S., often baptizes hundreds of candidates simultaneously for "entire sanctification" in outdoor pool at Newport News, Va.

➜

Religious education of children ranks high on program agenda of Christian groups. Catholic children, such as little girls (above), receiving communion from Father Thomas Pitsch in St. Paul's Church in Yakima, Wash., are educated in 10,000 parochial schools in U.S. alone. Protestant youngsters, like bright-eyed moppets (below) in Philadelphia Presbyterian Church, are trained in traditional Sunday School; Presbyterians recently spent $3,000,000 for colorful new *Christian Faith and Life* study series. 250,000 U.S. Sunday Schools now boast 2,000,000 teachers and 32,000,000 pupils, are in healthiest condition since 1900.

Brief as the teaching of Jesus appears, it covers every important department of life. How to give charity without show, how to pray, how to meditate, even how to conduct our worldly affairs with the single eye of faith. Man cannot serve both God and Mammon, he told his hearers, "but seek ye first the Kingdom of God, and his righteousness, and all these things shall be added unto you." Man is first of all a spiritual being—over and over Jesus tries to inculcate that. Other great Teachers have also tried to inculcate the same principle, but as yet few have learned it.

Above all, he preached kindness. "Judge not, that ye be not judged: For with what judgment ye judge, ye shall be judged." He preached the action and showed what the reaction would be. "Therefore all things whatsoever ye would that men should do to you, do ye even so to them: for this is the law and the prophets." Every great religion contains this, the Golden Rule, somewhere in its scriptures. But nowhere was it more simply stated than in the teaching of Jesus. Many of his precepts appear to us far too difficult to carry out. They appeared just as difficult, even impossible, to most men in his time. Yet to a handful of simple fishermen, tax collectors and the like, came the realization that the life he taught could be lived. And eventually those few blew the Roman Empire to bits. Peter was called the Rock, but virtually all of them shared in that adamantine faith. "Therefore whosoever heareth these sayings of mine and doeth them, I will liken him unto a wise man, which built his house upon a rock:

"And the rain descended, and the floods came, and the winds blew, and beat upon the house; and it fell not: for it was founded upon the rock."

The careless and disobedient build on sand and will be swept away by the first real storm.

The Golden Rule, loving your neighbor as yourself, divine compassion, purity of heart and mind, forgiveness and absolute love of God, these were the greatest among the teachings of Jesus. We are still very far from living up to them, but the road ahead is straight and open.

In Greek tragedy, one who commits a grave crime, like parricide or matricide, is pursued by the Furies, supernatural beings seeking to avenge the inhuman deed. In the life of Jesus, which culminated in the world's greatest tragedy, not supernatural beings, but earthly men full of fear, suspicion, intolerance, pursued the bringer of the best message men in those parts and times had yet received, and hunted and persecuted him even unto death. He jarred on narrow minds. "The Sabbath

In Europe, as in the Americas, Christian children sing and study stories of Old and New Testaments, participate in plays and pageants reenacting life of Savior. Girls and boys in Paris (above), shepherded by Sisters of Charity, descend steps of beautiful Madeleine Church as part of Easter Sunday processional in French capital.

In U.S., Protestant youth assembles each Sunday evening in such traditional fellowships as Christian Endeavor, Luther League, Baptist Training Union, and Liberal Religious Youth. Leaping denominational boundaries, Christian Endeavor alone numbers 3,000,- 000 members. Warren Hamilton, high school senior and president of West Hartford, Conn., Methodist youth (above), is typical of teen-agers who lead classmates in prayer, discussion, Bible-reading. YMCA and YWCA encourage same devotional spirit beyond school years.

was made for man, not man for the Sabbath." Some of his disciples, rough men of toil, forgot to wash their hands before sitting down to eat. That was so objectionable to the pious, it was tantamount to sin. The view Jesus took was: "There is nothing from without a man, that entering him can defile him: but the things which come out of him, those are they that defile the man." Talk like that sounded subversive to conservative authorities.

Besides, this Jesus of Nazareth ("can anything good come out of Nazareth?") was getting an ever-greater following. Speaking to a few people, he might be harmless. But crowds are a different matter. They might assume political as well as social significance. John the Baptist had to be liquidated when he was in the way of becoming too popular. They began to send out spies to listen to Jesus and, if possible, to catch something politically dangerous in his talk. They began to spread rumors that he had an evil spirit, whatever that might be. The revolutionary Zealots would have none of him because he was against revolution. The narrative tells how

he privately informed the disciples of his mission, how he must make his way to Jerusalem, regardless of the odds against him, and there face persecution, suffering and death, so that his mission might be fulfilled. Without haste, but without stay, with a determination that was more than human, in view of his expectation, he made his way to Jerusalem to arrive in time for the Feast of Passover.

The town was crowded with Jews come up from all quarters for the great festival. Pontius Pilate came from Caesarea to be on hand. People stayed in tents and even in caves. The Galileans, who had heard discourses by their fellow countryman at home, welcomed Jesus with cheers and shouts as he came riding down the Mount of Olives, accompanied by the dusty disciples on foot. People pointed him out to each other. "That? That is the new prophet, Jesus of Nazareth."

From then on, the remaining days of Jesus' life seemed to follow each other in a crescendo, like situations, scenes and acts in a play. He visited the Temple and drove out the dealers in sacrificial

Throughout world, Salvation Army applies "its heart to God and its hand to man" in moving demonstration of Christianity in action. Evangelical movement, begun by British minister William Booth in 1865, still has as its objective conversion of people everywhere to Christian living. International Army's drum and band boom out on Chicago's Skid Row (above), where cadets in training kneel in prayer with men who stopped for sidewalk meeting. Today, General Booth's dynamic Christianity is serving hungry, ailing people in 97 countries.

pigeons and overturned the tables of the money-changers, on the ground that their activities were sacrilegious in God's house. The priests and the Pharisees tried in turn to catch him in sacrilege. Jesus told them, among other things, "That the publicans and the harlots go into the Kingdom of God before you." He also told them that the Kingdom of God would be taken from them and given "to a nation bringing forth the fruits thereof." More and more he tempted them to take extreme measures. Jesus knew that his death was imminent.

He even knew who was to be his betrayer. There was the solemn rite of the Last Supper, and later, the betrayal by Judas in the Garden of Gethsemane to the henchmen of the high priest. "O my Father," he had prayed, "if possible let this cup pass from me. Nevertheless, not as I will, but as thou wilt." And again, "O my Father, if this cup may not pass away from me, except I drink it, thy will be done."

Arrested in the Garden, he was haled before the Elders, the Sanhedrin, and sentenced to death for blasphemy. Pilate, instead of carrying out sen-tence as the representative of Rome, sent Jesus to Herod Antipas, Governor of Galilee, who was in Jerusalem for the holiday. Herod returned the prisoner to Pilate. One capital prisoner was always released at this time by Pilate as a kind of grace, or amnesty. He offered to release Jesus. But the crowd shouted they wanted Barabbas released in-stead. He was a Zealot revolutionary. And so Jesus was remanded to the Cross, a favorite Roman punishment. And that Cross eventually destroyed the Roman Empire. The scourging with whips by the Roman soldiery, the Crown of Thorns placed upon his head in cruel derision, his dragging the heavy cross to Golgotha, the Hill of the Skull, to be there crucified between two thieves—those scenes have burned themselves into the minds of countless generations of devotees. Referring to the howling mob that reviled him, he said, "Father, forgive them; for they know not what they do"—surely, the most God-like prayer ever uttered by the lips of man. With a profound sigh he then committed his soul to God and expired.

"Wisdom cries aloud in the streets" today in New York's Wall Street, as in old Israel of Proverbs. Everywhere in U.S., evangelists like Church of Christ in God preacher give sidewalk sermons and witness for Christ.

From that moment, all that was essentially Jesus, the great soul, the divine Spirit whose gospel could be summed up in the single word, Love, began to live in a way no soul and no spirit had ever lived before. The story as told in all the four Gospels is, with only slight variations, identical.

Joseph, a faithful man of Arimathea, and a devotee of Jesus, had a certain influence with Pontius Pilate, the Roman Governor who had sent Jesus to the cross. Directly after the crucifixion he asked Pilate for the body of Jesus that he might give it decent sepulture. Pilate having complied, Joseph carried the body to the tomb newly completed for himself in his own garden and laid his friend to rest in the unused tomb. That was on a Friday toward dusk on the eve of the Jewish Sabbath. When Mary Magdalene and others came to the tomb early before sunrise the morning after the Sabbath, the tomb was empty. Christ, they reported to the other disciples, had risen and was nowhere to be found. Very soon they saw, they declared, his shining form in their midst. St. Paul, in his epistles to the Corinthians, tells with great precision how the risen Christ was seen first by Cephas, that is Peter, then by the twelve and still later by more than five hundred devotees, many then living. "And last of all," adds Paul, "he was seen of me also, as one born out of due time."

The vision Paul recalls in that sentence is one of the most important occurrences in Christianity, in all religious history. Convinced by events that Jesus was the true Messiah, and that he had come on earth to prepare for his second and more triumphant coming, his disciples clung together in Jerusalem and met daily for prayer and communion. The group included Mary, the mother of Jesus, James, his brother, and all the Apostles. That group meeting, as it is said, in an upper room in Jerusalem, was the true beginning and nucleus of the Christian Church. When they went out to preach in the streets people were amazingly attentive and impressed. When they were arrested, as both Peter and John were, their defense was, "We must obey God rather than men." They, unlike their fellow Jews, believed the Messiah, in the person of Jesus, had already appeared, and come what might they would spread that message.

Some of them, as for instance James, the brother of Jesus, and nearly all the Apostles, adhered to the orthodox Mosaic law. Others, however, who had lived abroad, Greek-speaking Jews, took a more radical view and scorned the rigid practice of the

**New Ministers,** representing 50 Protestant sects, line up at

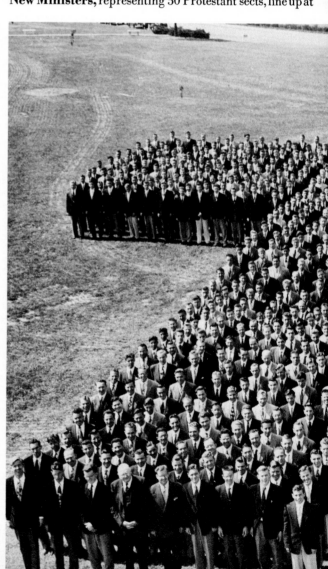

182

Sadducees and Pharisees. Liberal or orthodox, however, these new Christians were steadily persecuted, and no one was more relentless in their persecution than Saul, a Greek-speaking Jew of Tarsus, later known to the world as St. Paul. He had come to Jerusalem as a sort of university student, to study the Jewish law under the Rabbi Gamaliel. When many of the Christian believers left Jerusalem for Damascus, as a safer place for their doctrine, Saul of Tarsus followed them with all the zeal of an inquisitor. Then the great event of his life overtook him.

"And as he journeyed," we are told in The Acts, "he came near Damascus; and suddenly there shined round about him a light from heaven:

"And he fell to the earth, and heard a voice saying unto him, Saul, Saul, why persecutest thou me?"

"And he said, Who art thou, Lord? And the Lord said, I am Jesus whom thou persecutest."

He was blind for three days and fellow wayfarers led him by the hand into Damascus. In a few days, as his sight and his strength returned, he was preaching Christ in the synagogues and proclaiming him as the Son of God. But he was not only a

Commencement at Bob Jones University, Greenville, S.C.

Sister Mary Isnard of Sacred Heart Convent, Springfield, Ill., gets hit in game with St. Fidelis. Sister Mary Lambert is catcher. In such holy orders, nuns dedicate themselves to God, pray for salvation of all mankind.

preacher. He was a tremendous organizer. Wherever he came he created a center, a church. In Asia Minor, in the Greek world, all the cities were well known to him. His Epistles, or letters, to the Corinthians, Ephesians, Galatians, and so on, were the first written sections of the New Testament. He was zealous, daring and fearless. "The Lordship of Christ Jesus" was to him a talisman that accompanied him always and saw him through every danger. Persecution, prison, lashes, all were acceptable as part of his mission. And when, as a Roman citizen, he "appealed to Caesar" after being arrested in Jerusalem, to be shipwrecked at Malta, to be bitten by an adder, to be cast into a Roman prison, all was to him part of the day's work. From the prison he wrote a steady stream of letters to the churches he had founded. It is no wonder he has been called "the second founder of Christianity." Aside from Jesus himself, Paul was the greatest propagandist the Faith ever had. Jew, Roman, Greek and numerous other categories could unite in the community of Christ, and Paul was a powerful factor in that union. It was Paul, in short, who played the dominant part in making of a small Jewish sect a great world religion.

The epistles or letters of Paul had, as we have seen, preceded the Gospels. But sometime between A.D. 65 and 70, John Mark, a Christian of Antioch, wrote

Diversity in unity keynotes Protestant worship. Lutheran vestments and liturgy, although similar to Catholic forms, are based upon Luther's "salvation through faith" and God's Word. Confirmands (above) face altar in Minneapolis' Central Lutheran Church. Cathedral Choir of Los Angeles First Congregational Church (below) presents its annual Bach festival.

the Gospel that bears his name. It is probable that the actual year of its composition was 67, the year Paul was executed by the Romans. Christianity was an active, a widely spreading religion, and the Elders saw need of some written record. Between 70, the year Jerusalem was destroyed by Titus, and A.D. 100, the two Gospels of Matthew and Luke came into being. From the first, the writers of the Gospels refer to Jesus as a divine being. In the Fourth Gospel, however, the book of John, written about A.D. 105, Jesus is not only the Son of Man and the Son of God, but the Logos, the Word made flesh, one with God. The first three Gospels, Matthew, Mark and Luke are known as the synoptic Gospels, because so much of their material parallels or corresponds. In Mark, there are only thirty-one verses which are not in substance found in either Matthew or Luke. It is possible they all relied on some source, perhaps a Greek manuscript of Antioch, known to scholars as "Q," abbreviation for the German word *Quelle,* or source. That source is now lost. The Gospel of John, however, stands by itself. It is the most allegorical as well as the most mystical of the four Gospels and much of Christian theology stems from it.

By the second century, the Christians were already a problem to the Roman Empire. As early as A.D. 64 Nero was persecuting them and making victims of them in the Roman arenas. By the first quarter of the second century, Pliny the Younger, governor of Bithynia, was consulting the Emperor Trajan upon the subject of dealing with Christians. They underwent torture and martyrdom for Christ's sake without complaint, often, indeed, with alacrity. By the time the "good" Emperor, Marcus Aurelius, came to the throne in 161, he realized that the barbarians on the Rhine and the Danube could not be contained if the pacifist creed of Christianity was allowed to gain and flourish. He and a number of his successors therefore tortured, slew and burned many Christians in order to stamp out their creed. The worst persecution of all, under Diocletian, came in 303, when churches were burned, scriptures destroyed and bishops tortured, until it looked as though the end of Christianity had come. Yet only ten years later, a new Caesar, Constantine, was granting freedom of conscience to all, Christians as well as to followers of other religions, and before long he was building up the Church. It seemed like a major miracle.

In the year 383, Christianity was declared the imperial state religion of Rome.

That was a tremendous victory. What had made

it possible was the almost uninterrupted progress and growth of the Church in spite of persecutions, martyrdoms and deaths. As early as the middle of the second century there were churches in Persia, Media, Parthia and Bactria. By the third and fourth centuries, long before Christianity became the official religion of Rome, churches were numerous in Egypt, even the Coptic language being no barrier. There were churches in India, in North Africa, in Gaul, in Britain and even in Germany. All this in spite of the fact that to the unintelligent populations every plague, every famine, every earthquake and every flood was charged to the activity of the Christians, to their defections from the pagan gods. Yet, two hundred years after the conversion of Constantine, the power of paganism had vanished.

The Church Fathers, as the writers of the first six centuries of Christianity were called, were ceaselessly defining, expounding, commenting, starting and settling Christological controversies, with a warmth and heat characteristic of theological disputes. Feeling ran high. If a Nestorius of Constantinople declared that the Virgin Mary did not bear a deity, but "a man, the organ of deity," the monks of Constantinople broke out in riots and Nestorius was banished. Yet there are Nestorian churches even today in India and Iran.

A single word could cause intense argument and have a decisive influence in splitting the Church asunder into Eastern and Western branches, unreconciled to this day. Such a word was the Latin "*filioque*," meaning "and the Son." Augustine wrote that the Holy Spirit "proceeds not only from the Father but also from the Son (*filioque*). The theologians of the Eastern Church protested this on the ground that it seems to deny God as the source of everything. That difference persisted for nearly five centuries, until 1054, when the Eastern and Western churches separated permanently, Byzantium and Rome remaining forever apart.

Monasticism appeared early in the history of the Christian Church. As early as the third century a saint of Egypt, Anthony of Korma, retired into the desert to fight the temptations of the flesh that beset him. Many others followed St. Anthony into the desert, into caves, into trees, or even to the tops of pillars, like St. Simeon the Stylite. Before long, the hermits and those who would leave the world gathered themselves into monasteries for the life of contemplation, supporting themselves by their own labor in the fields and otherwise. The breakup of the Roman Empire sent many into monasteries for refuge. And some of the great orders like the

American Methodists, numbering nearly 12,000,000, worship in such unadorned meetinghouses as Greencastle, Ind., church (above), emphasize inner "witness of spirit" and social gospel. Protestant Episcopalians, who have 3,000,000 members in 7,500 parishes, cooperate in interfaith meetings like Southwest Convocation (below), where Texas Bishop Everett Jones is speaker.

Russian Orthodox communicant enters National Episcopal Cathedral in Washington, D.C., for Christmas service. America's "Westminster Abbey" welcomed 279,779 visitors last year. Russian parish, which has 55,000 members in U.S., is allowed to use famed church.

Catholic worshipers kneel in prayer before *Pietà* at St. Patrick's Cathedral in New York City. Sculpted splendor of Mary holding Jesus, as well as paintings and colored glass windows, are typical of interior elegance of many Catholic churches. "St. Pat's," a

Benedictines, Dominicans, Franciscans, Cistercians, played tremendous roles in the development of Christianity and European civilization.

Great and powerful personalities arose in the early centuries of the Church who contributed incalculably to the growth and expansion of the conquering faith. The fourth century in especial was rich in these great spirits. John Chrysostom of Antioch, John "of the Golden Mouth," was the most eloquent preacher of his time. From the pulpit of St. Sophia in Constantinople, he preached to vast audiences who carried his fame and message into all the Christian world. As an interpreter of Scripture and the truth of the Bible, he had at the time no equal.

Jerome, a Dalmatian, one of the great scholars of his time, translated the Bible into Latin, now known as the Vulgate. Its language, as one writer puts it, "formed the language of theology and letters throughout the Middle Ages." Both of those saints, Chrysostom and Jerome, led ascetic lives, surrounded though they were by luxurious living.

More famous even than these, however, was St. Augustine, born in North Africa, of a pagan father and Christian mother. Long before he became Bishop of Hippo he was a brilliant teacher of rhetoric and admittedly a confirmed sinner. His *Confessions* are still a best seller today, one reason being his absolute frankness about his sins of the flesh. Another is the vigor and nobility of his mind. How he became converted to the Christian faith is an episode almost as celebrated as the miracle of St. Paul on the road to Damascus. Augustine was sitting in a garden in Milan when he heard a voice insistently repeating in his ears, "Take up and read." The Epistles of Paul were lying on a table indoors. So he took up the book and his eye fell upon these words: "Not in rioting and drunkenness, not in chambering and wantonness, not in strife and envying; but put ye on the Lord Jesus Christ, and make not provision for the flesh to fulfill the lusts thereof." Those words changed his life. The Easter Sunday of the year 387 he was baptized by Bishop Ambrose at Milan. The following year

towering structure of modified Gothic, was designed by non-Catholic James Renwick and was opened to public in 1879. Its beautiful Lady Chapel was dedicated in 1906. Seating 2,300 persons, Fifth Avenue cathedral is head church of Cardinal Spellman's See.

Methodist minister Cassius Street conducts communion in Kansas City Linwood Church. Methodists, who recognize Lord's Supper and Baptism as two sacraments ordained of God, take bread and wine in "a spiritual manner" as sign of man's redemption through Christ.

he founded the Augustinian Order, pledged to poverty, celibacy, study and prayer. From then on, he became and has continued to be one of the greatest influences in the Christian Church.

Though the Roman Empire was rapidly dissolving, the Church was steadily increasing in strength. Church and State became more and more intertwined into what ultimately emerged as the Christian civilization. Clashes between kings and pontiffs were of constant occurrence. Nevertheless, a ruler like Charlemagne was of tremendous help to the Church. A pope could excommunicate a king, as Gregory VII excommunicated Henry IV of Germany, or Innocent III excommunicated King John of England and declared his throne vacant. That brought John to heel. But Henry IV of Germany later had opportunity for revenge when he marched upon Rome, drove Gregory VII out and deposed him as Pope. The Church, however, remained unshaken. It was not until Henry VIII of England and Martin Luther of Germany broke away from it that the Church suffered its sharpest division. But that took place centuries later.

The monasteries and the cathedrals that arose after Charlemagne (he died in 814) were establishing schools so that boys and young men might be taught what there was available of religious knowledge chiefly, but also bits of Aristotle, Plato and the writings of St. Augustine. Teachers began to compose texts and treatises. Clusters of students gathered round certain famous teachers. Universities were forming. Bologna for Canon law and Salerno for medicine, Oxford and Paris for theology. Out of these schools emerged Scholasticism. People still jestingly repeat the old story that a main problem of Scholasticism was how many angels can dance on the point of a needle. Some of the questions propounded and debated were no doubt puerile. But the great problem was to reconcile reason and revelation, much as today men still strive to reconcile religion and science.

Arabic texts of Aristotle coming out of Spain, where the Moors still held part of the land, were translated into Latin, and Thomas Aquinas, the flower of Scholasticism, built what amounted to a new theology in the light of Aristotelian philoso-

phy. His great works, *Summa Theologica* and *Summa Contra Gentiles,* are still the bases of Catholic theology.

Scholarship, clerkly knowledge, letters, were bound up with the Church. The Church was fortunate. A work of genius by a layman, Dante's *Divine Comedy,* suddenly illumined and dramatized all the close thinking of Thomas Aquinas, even as the appearance earlier of St. Francis sent a glow of light throughout Christendom. Chivalry was to such a degree held under religious auspices that a priest blessed the sword of the new knight before he received the accolade from the lord who knighted him. The Crusades were inspired by the Church. The violence and barbarities of the Crusaders, of which there were numerous instances, ill befitted their ideal, which was to regain the Holy Sepulcher for the Christian world. But, in any case, it brought the Crusaders and Europe in contact with another civilization. The Crusades failed to win Jerusalem, but Europe gained in culture.

The fall of Constantinople to the Turks in 1453, which drove many Greek scholars to Italy and France, bringing precious Greek masterpieces to Europe, started a revival of classical learning and the period that is called the Renaissance. It was literally a rebirth. Even popes and prelates became imbued with the new learning. It stimulated not only scholars and churchmen, but others as well, including the common man, to question, to appraise, to criticize. Were the practices of the Church all that they should be? Was the sale of indulgences, or remission of punishment of sins for money, in keeping with the teachings of Christ?

Martin Luther, a monk of Wittenberg who had begun as a law student, found this traffic in indulgences intolerable. He preached against it and, on October 31, 1517 (a notable date), he nailed to the door of All Saints Church in Wittenberg (Saxony) his Ninety-five Theses, telling what he thought of the practice of selling indulgences. That document was the beginning of the Reformation. Immediately war broke out between Luther and the Papacy. The German princes stood by him, however, and in the end he won his fight. As the Eastern Church separated from the Western in medieval times, so now the northern peoples of Europe separated themselves from the southern. Italy, France, Spain, remained Catholic. Germany, England, Scandinavia became irreconcilably Protestant.

Simple as that sounds, it was one of the important factors that gave rise to the Thirty Years' War, among the most tragic wars in history. The population of Germany is said to have been reduced by half, or even more than half. Europe was drenched in blood. Protestantism divided into many sects, and these in turn divided further.

Someone has declared that he wishes every human being were a sect by himself. Then religion would be truly alive. As the sects began to proliferate, after the Reformation, it seemed almost as though that would come to pass. They began to read the Scriptures intensively and to find new and imperative meanings hidden in the texts.

The Anabaptists, for instance, protested that infant baptism was meaningless. What can an infant know of baptism? So they had themselves rebaptized as adults. This, together with certain other beliefs about rituals and ceremonies, refusal to take oaths, to serve in the armed forces, and a leaning

Life of poverty, chastity and obedience, as well as lifelong silence, is embodied in cowled figure of Trappist monk walking to chapel in monastery at Cumberland, R.I. Both Catholics and Episcopalians maintain monasteries in America and Europe, ranging from purely contemplative to "mixed" groups combining prayer and outside work. Trappists, a branch of 17th-Century Cistercian Order founded in Normandy, wear brown habit, eat frugally, never marry. In service to man and love of God, they resemble monks of great Asian faiths.

Postwar U.S. religious revival has swelled numbers of such evangelistic sects as Disciples of Christ (left), Jehovah's Witnesses and Pentecostal Assemblies. Revivalists stress repentance of sin and Christ as Savior.

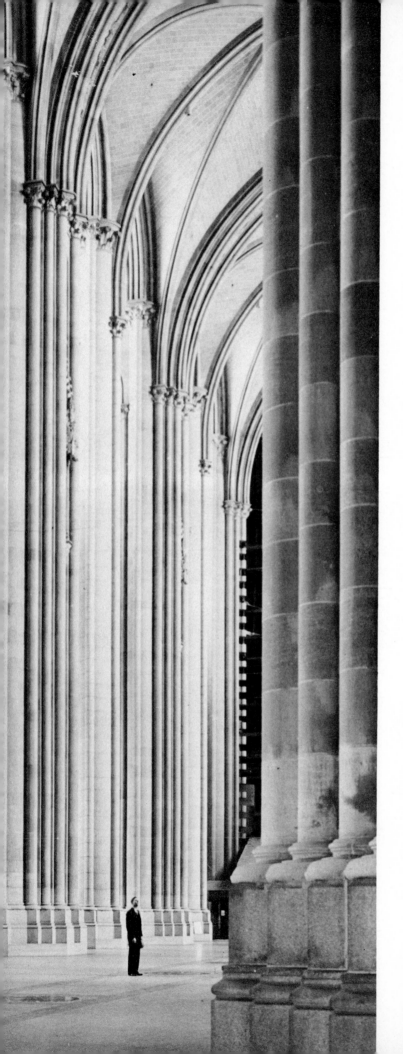

toward communistic life after the manner of the early Christians, sufficiently separated them from the rest of reformed Christendom to bring persecution, drownings and burnings at the stake.

From them, later, led by Menno Simons (born the year Columbus discovered America) came the Mennonites, a far quieter, though no less religious offshoot, well-known to us by their habit and customs, in the United States, notably in Pennsylvania. It was a Mennonite in Holland who gave refuge to Baruch Spinoza, that "God-intoxicated man," when both Jewry and Protestant Christianity alike ostracized him, because his creed was far too broad and inclusive for them.

In 1531 a man named Michael Servetus, or Miguel Serveto (he was a Spaniard) published a book called *Concerning the Errors of the Trinity*. His beliefs were Unitarian. He was tried in Geneva, the seat of Calvinism (Calvin condemned him), and burned at the stake in 1553. But Unitarianism is flourishing today. Similarly, the Universalists, who also find evidence in early Christianity for their belief that salvation is universal for man under a just and loving God, came into being in America about 1770. Today they are almost as numerous as the Unitarians and actually have more churches. They have founded four colleges and two seminaries, and are growing in activity.

Or take Congregationalism. In 1616, four years before the Pilgrims landed on Plymouth Rock, a church was opened in Southwark, London, dedicated to a new type of church organization. No bishops, no presbyteries, no hierarchy of any kind. Every congregation was to be an individual unit. Jesus Christ was the head of every such church. Some groups of the Anglican Church who despaired of bringing about reforms in the Church of England separated themselves from that, and even emigrated to Holland. They were the future Congregationalists and Baptists. It was the Puritans of the Church of England who came in thousands to Massachusetts and Connecticut and became the Congregationalists of those highly Congregationalist States.

The Baptists started their sect in London in 1612. Twenty-six years later, Roger Williams had a Baptist Church in Rhode Island and Baptism spread throughout the American colonies.

About this time in 1624, George Fox was born. His was a different kind of religious interest. By the time he was nineteen he was seeking spiritual enlightenment. By 1648, only five years later, he was preaching in market places, and wherever he could find an audience, about the *inner light* which

St. John the Divine, 64-year-old Gothic cathedral of Protestant Episcopal Diocese of New York, is the biggest church in U.S., holds 10,000 in its great nave, is seat of Bishop Horace W. B. Donegan. The Episcopalians are sixth largest communion in country.

←

is more important than sermons, and the "concern," without which Christianity is mere conformity. William Penn, as we know, the son of a quite blustery British admiral, embraced this gentle creed, and became the foremost benefactor of Quakerism. He persuaded "friend Charles," as he was wont to address King Charles II of England, to give him the grant of Pennsylvania, which became a refuge not only for Quakers, but for all religions. Today there are probably not many more than 150,000 Quakers in the world. But no sect carries more weight in welfare work than the Society of Friends, and none is more respected in both the Christian and non-Christian worlds. For to the true Quaker there is "that of God" in everyone, and to this every believer cannot help but respond.

Of late years we have heard much of the "Oxford Group," in connection with the very active movement toward moral rearmament launched by the former Lutheran clergyman, Frank N. Buchman. Well, there were Oxford groups, or movements, before now. Early in the nineteenth century there was an Oxford movement involving such great divines as John Henry (later, Cardinal) Newman, John Keble, and others in an effort to revitalize the Anglican Church. But a hundred years earlier, to be exact, in 1729, John and Charles Wesley, two brothers, and a third, George Whitefield, Oxford students, began meeting in their college rooms for religious and spiritual exercises, prayer and religious study. Those young men were no triflers or dilettantes. They resolved to conduct their lives and study by rule and method. Hence some of their contemporaries sarcastically referred to them as "Methodists." Actually those young leaders were ordained clergymen of the Church of England. But with the multiplying scientific discoveries, like those of Galileo and Sir Isaac Newton, and the beginning of the industrial revolution, religion had grown cold and conservative in the view of those young enthusiasts, who determined to revitalize it. They did. The Wesleys and Whitefield were amazingly persuasive preachers. People flocked to them. A new denomination was born. It became the Methodist Church. When the Wesleys first brought Methodism to Georgia, in America, it was not too successful. Upon their return to England, however, their crusade became overwhelmingly popular with the working people, and by the latter part of the eighteenth century it began to spread in America rapidly. Today the Methodist is the largest Protestant communion in the United States, with more than twelve million members, and some forty thousand churches.

Church of the Rosary, perched atop 900-foot hill in San Pedro, Azores, is one of smallest Catholic churches and a favorite stopover chapel for trans-Atlantic tourists. Built by popular subscription, tiny church is distinguished by its 150 "prayer" steps.

→

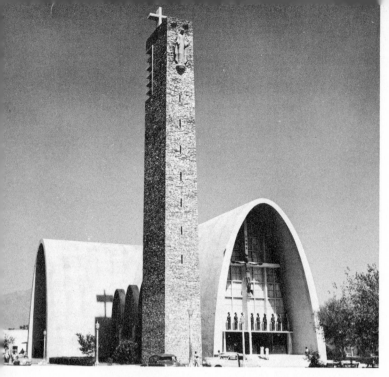

Church architecture is as varied as Christianity's "vast proliferation of sects." Radical design of Monterey, Mexico's new La Purísima Church (above) is oceans and centuries removed from Venice's domed and daz-zling Cathedral of St. Mark (above). Glittering glass and redwood Wayfarers Chapel at Portuguese Bend, Calif. (below), makes striking American church. Shrine is dedicated to Swedish mystic Emanuel Swedenborg.

First Church of Christ, Scientist, in Boston, "Mother Church" of nearly 2,000,000 members and 3,000 churches, was completed in 1906 under direction of discoverer of Christian Science, Mary Baker Eddy. Christian Science and Mormonism are the two major religions originating in U.S. First Universalist Church of Caribou, Me. (below), typical of New England's white-spired houses of God, represents free, non-creedal religion at its best. Universalists and Unitarians recently federated in a new Council of Liberal Churches.

"The family that prays together stays together" is the Christian adage faithfully followed by Mr. and Mrs. John Iliff and daughter Sheila Mae (above), who attend Miami's West Flagler Park Baptist Church. Sister of St. Mary (below) in St. Louis infirmary lovingly attends little child, for "of such is the kingdom of heaven."

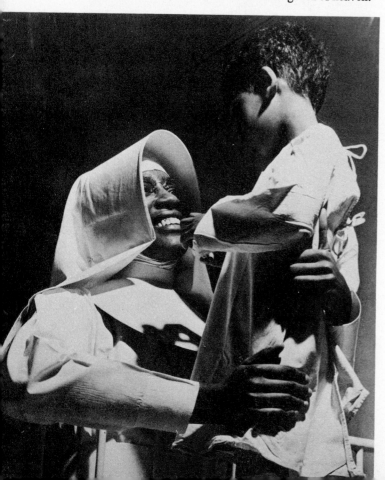

Such churches as the Protestant Episcopal, which is really the American version of the Church of England, the Lutheran Church which came to America with the early Dutch and Swedish settlers, and the Presbyterian Church of which John Calvin in Geneva, Switzerland, was the founder, are some of the other large sects with a membership of more than twelve million. Altogether, the Protestant bodies are said to have a membership of some fifty-five million.

The Catholic Church alone, in 1954, had a membership of nearly thirty-one million in the United States. After Martin Luther and Henry VIII of England launched the Reformation in Europe, a wave of inner reform swept the Catholic Church. One aim was to bring back the Protestants into the fold. But that proved impossible. Even to this day, however, pious Catholics pray for the conversion of all Protestants and, indeed, all the world, to the church for which is claimed an unbroken tradition going back to St. Peter and Jesus Christ. It is the largest church in Christendom and its adherents number hundreds of millions. To list all its dogmas here is neither necessary nor possible. But the supreme rule of the church is vested in the Pope, who is regarded as the direct successor of St. Peter. The church is endowed with infallibility, with the means of grace and the power to give absolution to sinners. The immaculate conception, the sinlessness and the virginity of Mary, Mother of Jesus, and the possibility of miracles, are some of the other dogmas of the church. The Holy See at Rome is actually a government, with its own foreign office, with representatives in sixty-seven countries, forty-three of diplomatic status, and twenty-four apostolic delegates. In days gone by it owned and governed a number of territories. But even today, Vatican City, the seat of the papal throne, is a state ruled by the Roman Catholic pontiff.

Sects, however, are not a Catholic phenomenon. There are in the Catholic Church certain *rites*, like the Armenian, the Rumanian or the Ruthenian rite. All, however, recognize the Roman pontiff as sovereign. It is otherwise, as we have seen, with the Protestants.

Today there are literally hundreds of sects. The activity of many of them in the missionary field has led to co-operation and even to talk of union. Thus, the National Council of the Churches of Christ in America has the support of thirty denominations. A pious hope of many a Christian is for an ultimate reunion of all Christendom. They still remember the momentous utterance of the Founder: "I and my Father are one."

Christian charity, which knows no national boundaries, is found amid flame and shadow, misery and want of every land. Protestant minister, conducting service in bombed-out Korean church, blesses bereft people: "The grace of the Lord Jesus Christ, and the love of God, and the fellowship of the Holy Ghost be with you all."

→

# 10. ISLAM

*There is no God but Allah and Mohammed is His messenger*

THE LAND WAS BARREN, BARREN as it is to this day. Even the date palm, so hardy and tolerant, does not prosper there. Mecca, from time immemorial a shrine for the people of the desert, is anything but alluring as a dwelling place. "Though the riches of three continents," says William Bolitho, "have poured ceaselessly into this wretched place, there are no gardens, and a stunted bush is a civic pride."

To be born into affluence in a place like that cannot mean much. To be born into austerity and an orphaned state can spell nothing but penury. Yet in 570, the man known to the world as Mohammed was born here of a young couple distinguished of ancestry, but poor in this world's goods, some two months after his father's death. One piece of luck he did have—he was born of an influential family. Though his mother died when he was six, he was taken into the home, first, of his grandfather, a man of seventy-six. When that tutelage ended, he was adopted by his uncle, Abu Talib, a very powerful man in Mecca, as was his entire clan, the Koreish. There was no real government in the city, and the strong clans and personalities arranged matters between themselves in a way that was mutually profitable.

And profits there certainly were. They came from the Kaaba. The Kaaba was an ancient Arab shrine with a mythical and reverential history. It was a quadrilateral structure, a cube—hence Kaaba—and it held the Black Stone that came from Heaven. Pilgrims from all Arabia came to Mecca annually, and they certainly carried no material wealth away from Mecca. But they brought a good deal. The Koreish and a few other families controlled all this traffic. The Koreish took fairly good care of their orphaned kinsman, Mohammed, but somehow it never occurred to them to teach him to read and write.

**JAMA MASJID OR GREAT MOSQUE** at Delhi is filled on

Fridays with 50,000 worshipers. On Moslem Sabbath, believers read Koran, eat at night, revere "God the Merciful."

With Koutoubia Mosque pointing to sky and Atlas Mountains shining in background, Marrakesh slumbers on its desert oasis. North Africa was converted to Islam within 30 years of Mohammed's death in A.D. 632 and within century Moslem Crescent extended from Spain to India. Prophet told Arabs, "All believers are brothers."

To the lad Mohammed, certainly unspoiled and early thoughtful, the story of the Kaaba itself was interesting. It was established, according to tradition, by Ibrahim, Father Abraham himself, when he came out of Ur. Near the Kaaba was a well—Zemzem. This well, too, had a great history. Do we not recall how Abraham's wife, Sarah, drove out Hagar, the concubine, together with her son, Ishmael? The child all but perished of thirst in the desert. Hagar ran back and forth distracted, in search of water. Zemzem was the answer. Ishmael was saved, and Ishmael is the ancestor of the Arabs.

For all their memories of Abraham, those Arabs were idolators. There were said to be 360 idols in the Kaaba. The Black Stone itself was at least a curiosity, a meteorite, that fell in some ancient day. But the idols—they could not have thrilled the more thoughtful of the Arabs. What Mohammed thought of them later, we know. He smashed them. But what he felt about them in his youth, we do not know. During his boyhood, he pastured sheep in the stony hills around Mecca. Then, his uncle, Abu Talib, took him, when he was only twelve, on a caravan to Syria. A camel boy's job is not easy. It meant his uncle had confidence in him. The city of Bostra in Syria, was not like Mecca, all Arab. There the boy saw Jews, Christians, perhaps even Zoroastrians. That may have opened his mind to the fact that men are not all idolators. This experience of his must have been repeated many times. For we suddenly hear of his taking a caravan himself to Bostra, for the wealthy widow Khadijah. For that operation, tradition says, he received in payment four camels. So well

198

*Solat* or ritual prayer is made by Arab soldier, who prostrates himself on blazing Jordan desert. One of five pillars of Islamic faith, prayer is performed five times daily at dawn, noon, afternoon, twilight, evening. Worshiper, who always bows low and faces toward Mecca, repeats Allah-praising phrases for 10 minutes.

did he acquit himself on behalf of the widow, so markedly did his reputation rise for trustworthiness and common sense, that Khadijah, through an emissary, offered him her hand in marriage.

The picture we get of Mohammed is that of a man of medium height, broad-shouldered, with a frank look, piercing eyes, a great head and a bushy beard. Perhaps that was later in life. For he was only twenty-five when he married Khadijah, though the lady was forty. At his death he was said to have nine wives. But during all the time he was married to Kadijah he lived a happy, monogamous life, even though polygamy was general. He had a number of children by her. Only the daughters survived and the best known of them was Fatima, the wife of Ali. For twenty-six years, until Khadijah's death, Mohammed and she lived together, and his grief at her death was great. She is described as a good woman, a good wife and a good merchant. But more important than all, she believed in him. She was his first convert and disciple.

For strange things began to happen to that solid, sensible citizen of Mecca, Mohammed, about the time he reached forty years of age. He had been much like other men, going to the Kaaba, presumably worshiping the idols, during the sacred month of Ramadan retiring to the solitude of one of the caves in Mount Hira for prayer and meditation. Though generally of a cheerful disposition, he fell at times into fits of melancholy. He was subject also to what was sometimes called "the sacred disease," that is, epilepsy. In any case, whether in trance, or fit, or dream, he saw a vision

In Cairo, *Mahmal* or Holy Carpet begins its annual journey to Mecca to fanfare of blaring bugles and crashing drums. Black velvet, gold-embossed carpet (right), which is one of series of coverings for Mecca's great "Kaaba" mosque, is borne in red and gold howdah atop elegantly-plumed camel. Accompanied by walking imams and mounted troops, Egypt's symbolic offering to Allah is carried through Cairo to city's edge where it is transferred to a camel caravan for 400-mile desert trek to Mecca. All-day ceremony, which is 700 years old, dates back to Queen Shagaret El-Dorr of Egypt who carried first carpet to Mecca. Its arrival today coincides with Courban Bairam Festival, commemorating Abraham's sacrifice of his son, Ishmael.

that left an indelible impression upon him and changed his life and the lives of countless others. An angel appeared to him in human form. He believed it was the Angel Gabriel, the same who spoke to Moses. The angel held a silver scroll. "Read!" said the angel.

"I cannot read," said Mohammed. Both the command and the answer were repeated twice.

"Read," said the angel again, "in the name of the Lord, who created man out of a clot of blood; read in the name of the Most High, who taught man the use of the pen, who sheds on his soul the ray of knowledge, and teaches him what before he knew not."

These opening lines, and all that followed in Sura 96 of the Koran burned themselves into Mohammed's mind. He believed and did not believe. Was he losing his sanity? He ran home to tell Khadijah, his best friend and most sympathetic admirer.

"Oh, Khadijah," he said, "I have never abhorred anything as I do these idols and soothsayers; and now verily I fear lest I should become a soothsayer myself."

"Never," replied the faithful wife; "the Lord will never suffer it thus to be."

She went on to speak of his many virtues, his common sense, no doubt, and general sincerity. She had a cousin named Warakh. She ran to him and told what had happened. "By the Lord!" exclaimed the old man, "he speaks the truth. It must be prophecy. He may be another Moses."

As to that, Mohammed paid little attention to it. Khadijah was a good woman, meant well, but she was his wife. She insisted she regarded him as a prophet. "Allah," she said, "will not suffer thee to fall to shame. Hast thou not been loving to thy kin, kind to thy neighbors, charitable to the poor, faithful to thy word?"

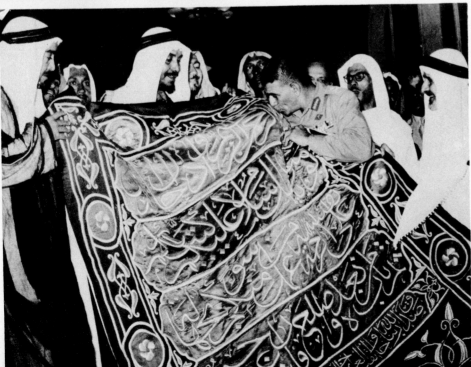

Egypt's Moslem President, General Mohammed Naguib (left), bends to kiss Holy Carpet before start of its shipment to Mecca. Verses from Koran, woven in gold and silver on black brocade, decorate magnificent tapestry which is created each year by the country's finest craftsmen at cost of $100,-000. Upon placing of new Carpet on Kaaba, the old one is cut up and pieces are sold to pilgrims for charity.

"Be faithful in prayer and give alms," Mohammed exhorted first converts 1,300 years ago. Today, 350 million Moslems pray with a faithfulness few religions can match. Nurtured by the desert's spaciousness and informed by its silence, North African Moslems deeply feel "everydayness" of God. With Pyramids of Gizeh as backdrop, Egyptian (above) kneels on Sahara for morning worship, while camel caravan (below) rests on Libyan desert near Tripoli for evening prayers. All worship is offered to "Allah, the Lord of Creation."

For all that, he was depressed. He went about moodily among the mountains, often thinking of hurling himself down from one of them. After a while he had another vision. He saw Gabriel again. The angel was seated upon a throne "between the heavens and the earth," and spoke to him: "O, Mohammed! thou art the Prophet of the Lord, in truth, and I am Gabriel." Mohammed went home in an exalted mood. After that, revelations came thick and fast. They make up the Koran.

There is a large collection of traditions, or *Hadiths*, relating to all of Mohammed's life and not least to this period of doubt, self-questioning and exaltation. Several months elapsed. But the rhapsodic revelations kept pouring from his lips in language he had not been accustomed to use. He had converts early—three—Khadijah, cousin Warakh, and Zaid, a former slave he had freed. No great showing this, but nevertheless Mohammed was convinced he was a *rasul*, a true prophet of God. Those *suras* he was uttering made sense. They were in scriptural language. That is how the Jews and the Christians got their scriptures. Why not the Arabs?

In three years of preaching and exhortation he attained only fourteen followers. His fellow townsmen of Mecca would have none of him. To them he was a byword, that "son of Abdullah, who hath his converse with the heavens." "A driveller, a star-gazer, a maniac-poet." There he was, in the courtyard of the Kaaba, breaking out, "In the name of Allah, the merciful, the compassionate." He seemed to be forever harping on a judgment day when the dead shall rise, and there were threats, too, of a consuming fire, a dreadful time, as set forth in Sura 81, the Overthrowing:

> When the sun is overthrown
> And when the stars fall,
> And when the hills are moved,
> And when the camels big with young are
>     abandoned. . . .

it was then the sky would be rent, hell-lighted. It was then every soul would know what it had produced and would have to stand its trial. When asked why they were cast into hell, the sorrowful souls will say, "It is because we were not of those who prayed, or fed the poor, and we rejected as a lie the day of reckoning."

The public trouble this man was causing was growing serious. It was not that they, the Meccans, minded his jeremiads, but the Kaaba with its idols was an attraction that drew pilgrims from all Arabia. The pilgrims brought money to the town.

In mystic silence, Arab Moslems sit in mosques in Medina (above) and Jerusalem (below). Worshipers leave shoes at door, kneel on rugs covering entire floor, face beautiful arabesque niche indicating direction of Mecca, birthplace of the Prophet in A.D. 570.

If the beliefs of these pilgrims were shaken, it meant no more pilgrimages and no more livelihood. Something must be done to silence this man.

It was not that Mohammed did not try to placate them. At one time, tradition tells, he gathered together forty of the most important members of his clan. He told them with the utmost earnestness that what he was preaching was of supreme importance to them and all mankind. Would they not back him in it? The only respondent to that appeal was his cousin Ali, the son of Abu Talib, a sixteen-year-old boy who became his convert for life and death. No one else came forward—not one. Indeed, when Mohammed was preaching, his uncle, Abu Lahab, a fat squint-eyed Arab, joined the listeners and shouted, "Believe him not, he is a lying renegade."

Others tried to break up the gatherings by throwing dirt and scurrilous insults at the speaker. But worse things were to come. His uncle, Abu Talib, his foster father and protector, died. He and Khadijah, the devoted wife, died within five weeks of each other. Some of the Hashimites, the branch of the Koreish to which Mohammed belonged, were beginning to weary of defending him simply because he was of their blood. To them, as to the rest of the town, he was a major nuisance.

One gleam of hope lay in the direction of Yathrib, some eleven days' camel journey from Mecca. During the four-month period of truce, a sort of truce of God, to enable people to make pilgrimages without being robbed, or killed, Mohammed had come in touch with some men from Yathrib. Their city, owing to blood feuds and vendettas, was in a state bordering on anarchy. A man of seeming authority, like Mohammed, they thought, with a religious accent, might be able to establish a decent government there. They agreed to lay the groundwork for the Prophet's arrival. Next time the Yathrib pilgrims came to Mecca they reported progress, and the next year they told him they were ready for him.

The problem for Mohammed was how to get there. That it was the place for him he felt sure. The people wanted him. There were many Jews in Yathrib, and they urged him to come. Besides, was not their religion, too, first announced by Abraham, the ancestor who worshiped the One God? Decidedly, Yathrib beckoned. But he knew his fellow tribesmen, the Koreish, and particularly the branch called Ommayads, under the leadership of Abu Sufyan. He had but to hint at moving, and they would strike him down. The news of his impending flight did actually leak out, and it was

Arms outstretched in supplication, Moslem women pray toward sun rising over Himalayas and vale of Kashmir. Prayer period occurs before weekly visit to mosque on Hari Parbat hill in Srinagar near Tibetan border. In India alone, Moslems number nearly 50 millions. All

decided to slay him. To avoid the annoyance of a blood feud, the conspirators agreed that at least forty families should be represented at his execution. To carry on forty feuds for one man was an unlikely occurrence.

But neither was Mohammed caught napping. One of his earliest and most devoted converts was Abu Bekr. The devotion of Abu Bekr is part of Islamic history. He helped the Prophet escape. When the conspirators reached Mohammed's home they found him flown. Young Ali was lying, seemingly asleep, in Mohammed's bed. Sleepily he told them what they already knew, that Mohammed was away from home. A frantic pursuit failed to discover either Mohammed or Abu Bekr. The shrewd Prophet was cleverer than his pursuers. Instead of riding in the direction of Yathrib, where he would certainly be overtaken, he and his

over Far East and Middle East, millions more are flocking to Islam's banner of brotherhood. With its emphasis upon charity, righteousness and good deeds and with no color line, collection plate or priesthood, Islam is fastest-growing religion in world today.

disciple went in the opposite direction and hid in a cave on Mount Thaur. When the hue and cry died down and the pursuit slackened, trusty friends brought a pair of fast camels to the cave and the two fugitives made the journey of some three hundred miles, which ordinarily takes eleven days, in eight days.

That was the *Hijra*, which is often called the Hegira, the flight, A.D. 622, and Mohammedan calendars call it the Year I. The city of Yathrib itself was renamed. It was called Medina, *the City*, that is, the city of the Prophet. It is worth noting that of those left behind by the fugitives, Abu Bekr's daughter and later Mohammed's young wife, Ayesha, the youth Ali and the Prophet's daughter, Fatima, none were molested by the men who had conspired to slay Mohammed. As reckoned today, the *Hijra* took place June 20, 622.

Tradition, needless to emphasize, surrounds this advent with many details and a great deal of circumstance. How the streets of Medina echoed with the cry, "He is come! He is come!" How a host of followers met and surrounded the Prophet, and seventy horsemen came forth and escorted him. The inhabitants cried, "Alight here, O prophet!" But Mohammed simply replied, "Let the camel decide." The camel, Al-Kaswah, moved on through the city and its gardens (Medina was not like Mecca) well into the southern part of the city, entered the courtyard of a date-drying barn, and there squatted and came to rest. That date barn became the first mosque of Islam.

There was almost every reason why that venture of Mohammed's should fail. It proved, however, to be one of the world's greatest success stories. The man who had fled his native city, harassed by people who wanted to take his life, arrived at another city, scarcely three hundred miles away, to become its head, the ruler of a state, the founder of an empire. Whatever his fellow townsmen ridiculed in him became the accepted gospel of all the Arab world. This was the beginning of a theocracy, on a scale the like of which the world had not seen. Modest though his beginning was, it proceeded with a firmness and a vigor hitherto unknown in the desert countries. Islam, the "surrender," had come into being. A new world power was born.

A definite religious procedure was quickly developed. The Christians had Sunday, the Jews had Saturday. Therefore Friday was appointed by the Prophet for weekly religious services. Five prayers daily, with every believer prostrating himself toward Jerusalem, at first; but later, when the Jews of Medina stubbornly refused conversion, toward Mecca. That prayer goal was called the *Kiblah*. Alms, or contributions for the poor and for the Prophet's maintenance, were regularly collected. Bilal, a powerful black convert from Abyssinia, once a slave, called the faithful to prayer from the rooftops every morning.

*"Allahu Akbar!* Allah is Mighty! . . . Prayer is better than sleep! . . . There is no god but Allah, and Mohammed is his Prophet." The call of the muezzin still resounds from the minarets of every Moslem land. A great mosque was begun in Medina. Before Mohammed's death a number of mosques were built, but the first one, the date barn, remained a sacred edifice. Here were delivered the new revelations of the Koran as they came to the Prophet's lips from Allah. The suras uttered at Medina became broader, not so much

Marriage, in far-flung Moslem Crescent, is as holy as in Judaic-Christian West. But, unlike Westerners, Moslem parents often betroth children before they are teenagers. Fatma, 8, dressed in pink satin pajamas, veil and gold earrings, and Mohammed Ali, 11, are "married" (above) in Pakistan state of Swat. After the ceremony, a band plays, the crowd cheers, and little Fatma is carried in sedan chair to Ali's home. Although bride will live at his house periodically, marriage will not be consummated until they are 16.

bent on individual guidance as on larger social and political problems. For politics was now a mushrooming factor in Islam.

The Prophet had signed a solemn treaty with the Jews of Medina, many of whom had a share in bringing him there. It provided for equal rights of citizenship and full religious liberty. Many writers point out the close resemblance of parts of the Koran to the Hebrew and Christian scriptures. One of the early suras, the third, includes this revelation:

"We believe in Allah, and in what has been revealed to thee, and to Abraham, and to Ishmael, and to Isaac, and to Jacob, and the tribes; and what was given to Moses and Jesus and to the prophets from Allah; nor make no distinction between them."

Well, if high angelic authority put the revelations of Mohammed on a par with what had been given to Moses and Jesus, and no distinction between them, then why did the Jews object to conversion to Islam, as most of them did? They were still patiently awaiting their Messiah. Not only Mohammed himself, but some of the Jews who supported him agreed that the Prophet was a possible Messiah. After all, he had paid the Hebrew Torah the greatest compliment. He had borrowed from it liberally. But a Messiah, it was insisted, must be not from the house of Ishmael, but from the house of David, and, as one writer put it, the Davidists won.

The followers of Islam needed arms, money, sustenance. Only a few of the refugees from Mecca could make a livelihood in Medina. An experienced old merchant like Abu Bekr could turn a penny by selling cloth in the bazaar of Medina. Omar, afterward a caliph, also did a little haggling in the market, and Othman, another future caliph, became a fruit vendor. Most, however, had no occupations and something must be done for them. The Prophet himself was poor. His wife, Ayesha, afterwards related that months would pass without a fire in the house. Their fare was dates and water. There is one method of obtaining supplies that has long been practiced in the desert, and that is robbery. Charles Doughty in his *Arabia Deserta* tells of the *ghrazzu* in the latter half of the nineteenth century. The raid, the foray, had its own laws and its own ethics. For, as Lawrence of Arabia cried, mimicking a certain powerful sheik, Motlog, "The land was barren—barren!"

Some tentative forays were made early in the Medina adventure, but without much result. With some tribes the Prophet entered into alliances, idolators though they were. But not with the Meccans. To these he was unforgiving.

A caravan belonging to Mecca was returning from Syria. Its leader, Abu Sufyan, caught a rumor that he would be attacked from Medina, and he sent a fast camel rider home appealing for help. Mohammed's force, a sorry assortment of 313 ill-armed men, reached a certain well or Water of Badr.

*Nikkah* or wedding ceremony unites modern Moslems in London service remarkable for its lack of music, cake or champagne. Marriage, solemnized according to Prophet's laws, is conducted in Arabic with imam reading from Koran. Before ceremony, groom's hair is rubbed with jasmine oil (above) and bride and mother share customary cry. During marriage rite, imam joins hands of Syeda Hussain and Mohammed Khan (below), blesses them, "Your vows to love, honor and obey are not made to yourselves only, but to God."

Women, whom Prophet considered "more valuable than all that is," play varied part in Islam now extending from Morocco to Indonesia. Generally, their legal lot compares favorably with Western women. In Rabat, Moroccan wife (above) pours tea, while in Karachi Pakistan leader offers thanksgiving during Bakr-Id Festival.

There they heard that the army of the Koreish was approaching. Abu Sufyan turned his caravan away from the direction of Badr. The Koreish troops and Mohammed's faithful met, while the Prophet under a shelter put up for him in the rear, was praying, "O Allah! If this little company is destroyed, there will be none left in the land to worship thee." Then he went into a trance, and when he came to, he told Abu Bekr that all was well. The help he had asked had come. And truly, the tide of battle turned. The Moslems fought like lions. They had Mohammed's promise of Paradise. Many of the most important men of the Koreish had fallen. Many prisoners were taken, and their baggage, weapons and camels fell to the Moslems. That was the Battle of Badr. Henceforth, there was a bitter blood feud between him and Mecca.

The Meccans were determined to wipe him out once and for all. In the year 5 of the *Hijra*, the Koreish with all the clans they could enlist, including a certain powerful desert tribe of Ghatafan, an army of ten thousand men, rode and marched upon Medina. What the Prophet felt at this threat we do not know. But a certain Persian named Salman told him how a great trench dug about the city might stave off defeat. Trench warfare, clearly, has a longer history than we might suppose. To the free-roaming Arabs of the desert, this device was utterly unknown. It was impassable to cavalry, and that was the chief strength of the assaulting army. The obstacle of the trench dampened the ardor of the clans. They were used to fast action and quick results. A fierce wind blew in from the sea. For three days not a tent was safe, not a fire could be lighted, nor a pot boiled. The leader of the Koreish ordered retreat. This was considered a miraculous victory.

In January, 630, the eighth year of the *Hijra*, Mohammed, now much strengthened, marched with ten thousand men upon Mecca. He took it almost without resistance. By then he was recognized as the greatest chief in Arabia. And where military prowess was so renowned, the spiritual side took on a new prestige. He acted with great magnanimity toward the conquered, and only a few were excluded from amnesty.

Almost his first act was to go to the Kaaba. What was he going to do—destroy it? On the contrary. He rode seven times around the Kaaba, even as pilgrims ran seven times around it. What of the Black Stone? He saluted it with reverence. Clearly, these were being shrewdly adopted into Islam. But there were the idols. Those he ordered brought out into the open and stood along the wall of the Kaaba. He pointed first at Hobal. "Truth is come!" he shouted, whereat a Negro with a huge ax broke the great idol to pieces. With his staff he pointed to the next idol, and the next, all were "executed," all the recipients of Arab prayers for hundreds of years. Tradition says those idols "screamed and sobbed." And well they might. For that was the end of idolatry in the Semitic world. He once again made Mecca the religious capital of all Arabia.

Mohammed announced himself to chiefs of states as the ruling head of the Arabs. What was he? A king, an emperor? He was told letters to high places must be sealed with an official seal. So he had a seal made which bore the inscription, "Mohammed the Apostle of God." Let the neighboring monarchs make what they would of that. The Emperor of Bzyantium, the Emperor of Persia, the Governor of Egypt, the Satrap of Syria, each received a letter announcing that the Messenger of God was one of them. The Emperor of Persia, it is told, tore the letter to bits. "Even thus, O Lord, rend his kingdom from him," said Mohammed, when he heard of it. The Governor of Egypt, by way of reply, sent the Prophet two Coptic slaves, beautiful young girls, one of whom presented the Prophet in his old age with a little son, Ibrahim.

The swiftness with which he consolidated all that became the Islamic Empire is one of the miracles of history. The Jews who refused to accept him as the Messiah, or his creed as theirs, he largely destroyed. All opponents, indeed, if they dared show resistance, were conquered by the sword. More distant tribes were "invited" to send delegations bringing their allegiance. That Arabia was unified, that idolatry was stamped out, that the people of the desert were morally elevated by his creed, no one can doubt.

His religious creed was uncomplicated. *La ilah illa Allah*—there is no God but Allah. As with the Hebrews, the declaration of the Unity of God was the most important article of the creed. He objected to Christianity because there, he said, "God is the third of three." His God was very personal indeed. At any time on any subject, He sent the Prophet a revelation and the next sura gave exact instructions for the disposition of a problem. The next important part of the creed is: *"Mohammed rasul Allahi,* Mohammed is the Prophet of God." Mohammed is the latest and greatest of the Prophets, according to his followers, and his is the most perfect, most complete of all the revelations. The Prophet disclaimed ability to perform miracles. He was human like other human beings, fond of

In socially-backward areas such as Sanaa, Yemen (above), women still wear *purdah* or veil when outside home. In Colombo, Ceylon, on other hand, Moslem ladies (below) display finery as they climb Adam's Peak to visit mosque. "Whoso knows himself, whether man or woman," say mystic Sufis, "knows his Lord."

**TAJ MAHAL AT AGRA**, acclaimed for 300 years as world's noblest building, was built by Mogul emperor Shah Jehan

as white marble tomb for his wife, Mumtaz Mahal.

Islam's "marble jewel" and grandest achievement of Moslem art, the Taj's construction required 20-year labors of 17th-century India's best architects and 20,000 workmen. The monument stands in a spacious garden (left) of green turf, cypress trees and still waters. Its great white dome is balanced by four smaller domes and four perfectly-proportioned minarets. The massive portals (below) and rich interiors are inlaid with semi-precious stones and decorated with colorful geometrics peculiar to Moslem art. Both Shah and the woman he immortalized are buried here.

Shi'ite sect of Islam, like zealots of every world faith, practice mortification of flesh as means to purification. Each September, Moslems honor memory of Mohammed's martyred grandson, Hussain, with flagellation ceremony. Ikon-bearing girls (above) lead procession.

Penitential parade through Zanzibar in British East Africa typifies observance of Hussain's martyrdom. Wielding barbed chains and chanting "Hussein, O Hussein," youths flail themselves until blood runs.

perfume and women, said Ayesha, nor did his followers ever deify him. The Koran is the final word of God to man. It has existed (in Heaven until given to Mohammed) from eternity. The Jewish and Christian scriptures are admittedly important, but not final, like the Koran. The angels are numerous, the chief being Gabriel, who conveyed the revelations. There is a devil and a Hell in Mohammed's theology. The Last Judgment is presented much as in Zoroastrianism. Transgressors will burn in Hell and cry out for water. But the pious will be "in a secure place, amid gardens and fountains," clad in richest silks. Comely youths will serve them with goblets of wine, the kind that will bring no one a headache.

And theirs shall be the Houris, with large dark eyes,
Like pearls hidden in their shells,
In recompense for their labors past.

The Five Pillars of Islam are the creed, prayer, almsgiving, fasting during the month of Ramadan, and Pilgrimage. At least once in a lifetime every Moslem must make the pilgrimage to Mecca. That *hajj* pilgrimage is said to antedate Mohammed by hundreds of years. Today the pilgrims continue to come from all quarters, from all over Africa, from Syria, Turkey, Iraq, Indonesia, India, by train, by ship, by plane, hundreds of them, thousands of them. When Charles M. Doughty made the journey with the *hajj*, starting from Damascus, he describes how 6,000 men and at least 10,000 animals, at the shot of a cannon, started off like a long, two-mile serpent, winding across the baking desert, most men mounted on camels, dromedaries, mules or donkeys, the drivers trudging on foot. The *Emir el-Hajj*, commander of the host, is riding in the van, and woe to him who falls behind or out of the caravan. At nightfall, the hajjies halt and, after a sparse meal, lie down in their clothes for a few hours' rest. At half-past five the next morning the cannon shot rings again and the weary march is resumed. A recent writer, who had made the trip by airplane, tells of all but unbearable hardships in the heat of Mecca, with more than 50,000 people crowded together in a small place. Some of the rites take place in the Valley of Afrat, where Adam and Eve supposedly found themselves after expulsion from Eden. The heat rose to 127 degrees Fahrenheit. On the second day at the village of Mina, where 150,000 sheep were sacrificed, the air became unbearable. The heat rose to 142 degrees. It was learned that 4,411 pilgrims had perished since dawn. Good Moslems, however, will not be deterred from making the *hajj* pilgrimage.

For Islam means "surrender," submission to Allah, hence to his Prophet and to the Koran, his book. And the book begins, we recall, as does every sura in it, with the words: "In the name of Allah, the merciful, the compassionate." That ideal has by no means exhausted its utility today.

The ninth year of the *Hijra* is known as the Year of Deputations. From all Arabia they came to swear allegiance to the Prophet and his Book. In the tenth year, the Prophet made his last pilgrimage to Mecca. There, in the revelation that is reckoned Sura 110, he is said to have received the first intimation of his approaching death. Many have blamed, and to this day blame, Mohammed for the bloodshed, the slaughter of the Jews and innumerable of his own kinsfolk. Yet, even outside of Islam, he is not without defenders. Among these is no less than the Sage of Chelsea, Thomas Carlyle. "You take wheat," he says, "to cast into the earth's bosom; your wheat may be mixed with chaff, chopped straw, barn sweepings, dust and all imaginable rubbish; no matter; you cast it into the kind, just earth; she grows the wheat—the whole rubbish she silently absorbs."

Others recall that Charlemagne, the Great Christianizer, killed 4,500 Saxons while converting them. Upon the other hand, Mohammed's humanity and kindness are brought forward. Sura 6 of the Koran declares: "There is no beast on earth, nor bird which flieth with wings, but the same is a people like unto you." It is pointed out that Christianity had been known in Arabia for 300 years and it failed to overthrow idolatry. Mohammed overthrew it in a single lifetime. Mohammed's love of children is cited, his provision in the Koran for widows and orphans, the humane treatment of women. He had brought the teaching of brotherhood to Islam and equality of all the faithful. To people accustomed to robbery, he preached that property must be respected no less than life. He put an end to idolatry.

The tenth and last year of the *Hijra* was upon him. It was his own last year on earth. His little son, Ibrahim, by the Coptic slave, died at the age of eleven months. That was a harsh blow to the Prophet. He had no other sons. His two grandsons, children of Ali and Fatima, Hasan and Husain, were the delight of his last days. On June 7, 632, barely ten years after his flight from Mecca, the Prophet died of a fever in the room of his favorite wife, Ayesha. He had come to Medina a fugitive. He died there virtually on the throne of an empire.

Who would succeed Mohammed was naturally the major problem of Islam. Often empires break

Istanbul, "the sublime porte" on Golden Horn, boasts pointed minarets, perfect domes and blue-green tiles of dozens of temples such as Dolmabache Mosque. It was built by Sinan, greatest of all Moslem architects.

→

Mausoleum of Emperor Akbar, 16th-century soldier-mystic, remains at Agra as symbol of Mogul empire extending across India. Noble monarch, who recognized Sikhs and reconciled Moslems and Hindus, had engraved over gateway, "God is great. There is no god but God."

up on the rocks of succession. Theocratic Islam avoided this danger for several centuries. Abu Bekr, who had often taken the Prophet's place at religious services, was the first of the *caliphs,* or "successors." He was a sterner ruler than might have been expected. He promptly punished attempts of tribes to break away. He "assembled" the Koran into permanent form and he dared to send an army against Syria, which meant against the Byzantine Empire. Omar, the next caliph after Abu Bekr's death, completed the conquest of Syria, took Jerusalem and Palestine, Egypt and North Africa. The incentive of the troops was un-beatable. If they lived, it meant loot. If they died, it meant Paradise. As Emerson points out, Omar conquered Arabia with only a bag of meal at his saddlebow. It was the same Omar who burned the library of Alexandria, one of the most irreparable losses mankind has sustained.

"If these books agree with the Book of God," said the caliph Omar, former huckster of the desert, "they are useless. If they disagree they are pernicious. In either case, they must be destroyed."

The great part of Asia Minor was taken over. The tide of Islam swept to the very back of the Himalayas, to Persia, to Spain, to France. Had

*Id-ul-Fitr* or festival ending fast of Ramadan is celebrated by massed thousands in Karachi park. Pakistani, like all good Moslems, stand shoulder to shoulder when praying to demonstrate democratic "togetherness" of faith. During Ramadan's great 28-day fast, Moslems do not eat, drink or smoke during day, but at night their households ring with sounds of feasting. Ramadan, like Jewish High Holy Days and Christian Lent, is also period of Scripture reading, self-criticism and dedication, forgiveness of wrongs, and prayerful submission to God who is "the first and the last, the seen and the hidden, the knower of all things."

In Isfahan, Iran's city of mosques, Shi'ites study Koran in Shah Masjid. The Koran, which means "to read," is at once book of prayer, prophecy and common law for millions.

Song of muezzin, echoing across Islam for 1,300 years, still is heard from Mecca minaret (above), calling pilgrims, "Come to prayer, come to prayer." Arab father (below), who has fulfilled life's ambition of making pilgrimage, joyfully dandles son in Holy City.

they not been stopped by Charles Martel at Tours in 732, all Europe might have become Moslem. To this day, many a church in southern Europe, in Sicily, for instance, is a transformed mosque, and the Alhambra palaces above Granada, in southern Spain, still attest not only to the wealth and luxury of the Prophet's successors, but also to the high civilization and culture they brought into Europe. Arab mathematicians, astronomers and philosophers ranked high at a time when the rest of Europe was still wrapped in medieval night. The Spanish-Arab philosopher Averroes, for example, in his great work *Commentaries*, on Aristotle, served European scholarship for a long time, and even St. Thomas Aquinas was a respectful student of the Moslem philosopher.

But even before the final expulsion of the Moors from Spain, in 1492, the Moslem Empire began to break up. The sweep of the Mongols, and the assault of the Ottoman Turks on Asia Minor and Europe, crumbled the empire apart into several small states. But the essence of Islam is still very much alive. Its followers are estimated to number about 350,000,000 in the world today. It is not possible here to speak of the various sects, such as the *Sunnis* and the *Shi'ites*, the *Hanifites* and the *Malakites*, the Shafites, the Assassins, the Mystics. To us, perhaps the most interesting are the mystics, or *Sufis*. In every religion, the mystics are the bond with every other religion. For theirs is the Perennial Philosophy—the knowledge that the Truth is One. One of the most famous of the mystical poets of Islam is Jalal-uddin Rumi, born in Balkh, in Bactria, in 1207. He was the founder of the Maulawi dervishes. In one of his poems he sings:

In the world of Divine Unity is no room for Number,
But Number necessarily exists in the world of Five
and Four.
You may count a hundred thousand sweet apples in
your hand:
If you wish to make One, crush them all together.

To the *Sufis* (the term means "wool-wearers"), there is only one quest, union with the Beloved—that is, God. Said Jalal-uddin:

"If the picture of our Beloved is found in a heathen temple, it is an error to encircle the Ka'abah: if the Ka'abah is deprived of its sweet smell, it is a synagogue: and if in the synagogue we feel the sweet smell of union with him, it is our Ka'abah."

All this is a far cry from raiding and robbing caravans.

Thousands upon thousands of pilgrims fill great courtyard of Mosque of Sanctuary, as twilight settles over Mecca. Object of their hearts' desire and end of their pilgrimage from all parts of earth, Mecca now shows faithful the birthplace of their Messenger and sacred Kaaba, a blue, carpet-covered building (above center)—"the most ancient edifice on earth and temple beside which Adam worshipped after his expulsion from Paradise." Here, in this historic shrine, Mohammed destroyed 360 false idols. Here, embedded in a corner of Kaaba, is venerated Black Stone, said to have been brought down to Abraham by Gabriel. Pilgrimage to Mecca, prayer, almsgiving, fasting, recital of Creed constitute five main duties of believers. Above all, Moslems must surrender to "God, the King, the Holy, the Peaceful, the Mighty, the Wise, the Most High."

New Baha'i Temple at Wilmette, Ill. is nonagonal white quartz edifice whose nine sides represent world's living religions. Baha'i house of worship, which bears inscription, "All prophets of God proclaim the same faith," crystallizes Assembly's belief in divine origin and unity of all major religions. Followers of 19th Century Persian prophet, Baha'u'llah, Baha'ists have 1,300 centers in U.S., 2,000,000 members in world.

Twelve Basic Baháí Teachings

1. The Oneness of Mankind.
2. Independent Investigation of Truth.
3. The Foundation of All Religions is One.
4. Religion must be the Cause
5. Religion must be in Acco
   Science and Reason.
6. Equality between Men and
7. Prejudice of All Kinds must be
8. Universal Peace.
9. Universal Educati
10. Spiritual Solution of
11. A Universal Lan
12. An International

# THE CHAIN OF
# THE TEACHERS

*Ye shall know the truth, and the truth shall make you free*

THE CONTINUOUS CHAIN OF THE teachers and teachings is one of the most striking facts of our life on earth. From earliest times, from prehistory, we see the procession of the Teachers, who cannot bear to leave their fellow men sunk in darkness. However heedless the race, those chosen guides who saw the Light cannot choose but share it with whomsoever they can persuade to accept it.

What is this light? What is the tremendous discovery they are so eager to impart? It is simply that God *is*. That He dwells in every human heart. However overlaid by what we in the West call sin, what in the East is called ignorance, there is within us a Being constantly seeking to shine through, to harmonize, to purify and to make us consciously whole. Nothing can stay the force and activity of that Dweller in the secret places of the heart. And sooner or later the greatest as well as the least among us comes to realize, in the words of Pascal, "The heart has reasons of which reason knows nothing."

Reason, however, is beginning to suspect that there are realms it has not touched. Science, we were told by Sir James Jeans, is not yet in contact with "ultimate reality." Nor is it likely to be very soon. But the heart knows, and its search, however hidden or unnoticed, never flags. That is why every Teacher who brings a gleam of Truth has at least *some* following. Certain of the Teachers have had followings of millions. The rate of growth varies, but delay in growth is not necessarily a sign of weakness. Many of the newer cults are still in possession of relatively few adherents, but, as we have seen in the histories of some of the great religions, numbers in the early stages are not a sure criterion of success or failure. Buddha's first converts were only a handful of ascetics. Mohammed

had but three or four at first, and for some time after his revelation Zoroaster had only one convert, his cousin. It is this absence of discouragement in face of seeming failure. and even persecution, that marks the Teachers of mankind, white milestones on the road to eternity. To name Hermes, Orpheus, Pythagoras, Lao-Tse, Confucius, Krishna, Buddha, Moses, Zarathustra, Jesus, Mohammed, is to mention but a few. Whether thousands of years ago or hundreds, there seems to be no end to the chain of the Teachers, and each of them had his particular message. Even in quite recent times some have made their appearance, with the same intrepidity and often the same results.

It was little more than a century ago that Mirza Muhammed Ali, the "Bab," as he called himself, the "gate" or forerunner of a new religion that should unite all religions and all peoples, was executed at Tabriz, in Persia, in 1850. What was his crime? As his successor, Baha'u'llah, phrased it: "All nations should become one in faith and all men brothers . . . diversity of religions should cease and differences of race be annulled." For this "heresy" he was executed. For a long time, Teachers have proclaimed those goals. For a long time they will go on proclaiming them. Baha'u'llah spent most of his life as a prisoner. So, for that matter, did his son, Abdul-Baha, who succeeded him. He was released only in 1908, when the Turkish revolution somewhat changed the complexion of the Near East. Where did he go upon his release? "I am going," he said, "to the United States . . . to proclaim the oneness of the world of humanity and the equality of all men." Men were galvanized by his spiritual power. A temple site was chosen at Wilmette, Illinois, and Abdul-Baha turned the first spadeful of earth for a million-dollar "Tabernacle of the Great Peace" and a center for Baha'ism. It is a fine and beautiful

Standing before Temple of Light, Baha'ist Dr. Hushang Javid of Teheran, Iran talks with National Assembly Secretary Horace Holley. Teaching basic oneness of mankind, Baha'i stresses progressive revelation of divine truth.

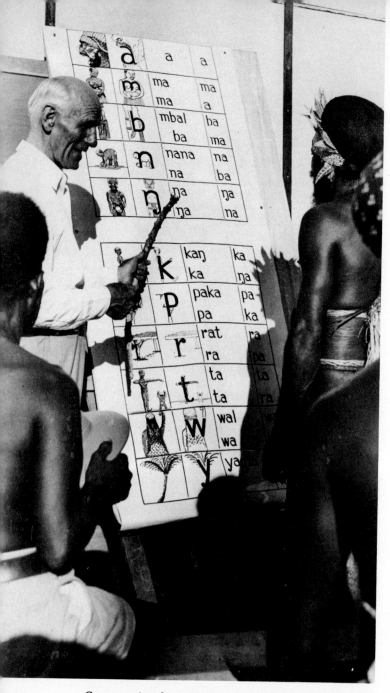

edifice, dedicated to the unity of mankind. Will the faith survive and grow and spread over all the earth, or will it remain a small cult? Who can tell? According to Mr. Horace Holley, Baha'i National Secretary, there are centers in 225 countries, with a total voting membership of 2,000,000. That can be called a rapid growth.

Similarly, Theosophy, first established by Helena P. Blavatsky in New York in 1875, has for its ideal a universal brotherhood of humanity, the study of comparative religion, the great philosophies, occult science, the secret doctrines. It was inspired by certain mahatmas in the Himalayas, and its ideals were of the highest. The goals set for the followers were, first, to purify hearts and minds, and then to make themselves over by the practice of concentration and meditation, as in the great oriental religions. It is safe to say that Theosophy has done more to spread an interest in Eastern religions and Yoga in the West than any single factor since Anquetil du Perron, a learned Frenchman, first brought the Upanishads from India to Europe early in the nineteenth century. According to the Swiss psychiatrist, Dr. Carl Jung, the spread of Eastern knowledge in the West is no accident. "No psychic value can disappear without being replaced by another of equivalent intensity."

In other words, the chilling of religious life in

Congregationalist missionary and mass educator, Dr. Frank C. Laubach, has taught 60 million illiterates, like New Guinea natives (above), to read and write. Combining Christian Gospel and picture charts, Laubach joins invisible choir of religious leaders who help cure world's ills by preaching love and sharing abundance.

Doctor, philosopher, theologian and often called world's greatest man, Albert Schweitzer exemplifies modern nobleman who "takes up his cross daily and follows Me." Nobel prize winner, who plays organ in African jungle station, runs Lambarene mission, heals ailing tribesmen, teaches a warring world "reverence for life."

the West does not mean the disappearance of religious feeling. The feeling is still there. So what was driven out through the door makes its appearance through the window—in the shape of Eastern religions, new cults and the priestlike practice of psychotherapy. Theosophy broke up into various sections. How many Theosophists there are today it would be difficult to say. But they are not as numerous as they were during the leadership of Annie Besant, whose commanding presence, great eloquence and strong leadership were powerful factors. Religions, however, have their ebb and flood.

One theosophist, Dr. Rudolf Steiner, an Austrian, separated himself from Theosophy early in the twentieth century to develop what he called a "spiritual science"—anthroposophy. He held this to be more suitable to the West than the oriental religions. Near Basel in Switzerland, at Dornach, stands the "Goetheanum," world center of Anthroposophy. While many of the members of the Anthroposophical Society are Germans, it has ramifications in other parts of the world, with schools, centers, publications, in England and the United States, as well as in other lands. To his followers, Rudolf Steiner was a great teacher, a fountain of wisdom. And, indeed, when one delves even a little into his many-sided knowledge and teaching, not

India's new "Gandhi" is 59-year-old Vinoba Bhave, a gentle, wispy ascetic who in three years has persuaded wealthy landowners to give 3,000,000 acres to the poor. Walking tirelessly from village to village, Bhave preaches sacrifice, devotion, non-violence, tells upper classes, "I have come to loot you with love."

Pope Pius XII, 262nd successor to St. Peter and Holy Father to 350 million Roman Catholics, leads Church's struggle against communism and moral corrosion. With Catholicism both triumphant and besieged, "Il Papa" calls upon Church to "become as a solid rock against which the fury of thy enemies will break in vain."

Mid-Century "revolt of the laymen" has intensified religious fervor in United States and Europe. Such groups as The Laymen's Movement (above), International Christian Leadership, Moral Rearmament, United Church Men and the Christophers quicken conscience of U.S., raise moral guideposts in business, increase daily religious awareness of millions. Leaders of Laymen's Movement, who presented U.N. Secretary General Dag Hammerskold (center) with leather-bound guest registers for U.N. Prayer Room, include president Wallace C. Speers (with Hammerskold), Ralston C. Young, famed "Red Cap 42" (left), Assistant Secretary General Andrew Cordier and Laymen's Executive Secretary Weyman Huckabee (right). Laymen's Movement was responsible for establishment of Prayer Room at U.N., as well as the institution of Laymen's Sunday.

only in the fields of philosophy and occultism, but in agriculture, medicine, chemistry, art, even in economics and politics, one cannot but wonder at the compass of his mind. Anthroposophy may not be a religion—its followers maintain it is not —but it certainly seems to make them more religious. Their colonies, wherever met with, whether in Europe or in America, are absorbed in better education, a less materialistic science, a richer, more intensive spiritual life. All the paths meet at the top. Steiner's combination of spirituality, occultism and science is perhaps the newest, and certainly the most original, of the paths.

It is not possible here even to touch upon all the cults and sects now in existence and, in many instances, flourishing. Who has not been impressed by Father Divine's Peace Mission Movement? Or the correspondence creed of "Psychiana," whose origi-nator, Frank B. Robinson, of Moscow, Idaho, claims to have talked with God—"actually and literally"? Who can enumerate them all? One is reminded of Queen Victoria's remark, when she first heard the message of Baha'ism:

"If this be of God, it will stand; if not, there is no harm done."

Queen Victoria was no divine, no theologian, no philosopher. Yet this utterance of hers was really an expression of wisdom—the wisdom of the race. Many cults have come and gone. Some have flourished and remain. Of the great religions, all, incidentally, of Asiatic origin, not one has perished. Zoroastrianism, to be sure, has not so much faded as dwindled, so small is the number of its followers today, compared with the time of its glory. But if we think of Hinduism, Buddhism, Judaism, Christianity, Islam, even Confucianism, all remain and,

Permanent World Parliament of Religions, organized in 1952 in New York City and pledged to promote greater understanding among world faiths, is working intensively to mobilize religious sentiment for peace and brotherhood. Through mass meetings, world tours and prayerful emphasis on truths uniting all races, Parliament meets new needs of 20th Century man. Speakers at organizational meeting at Presbyterian Labor Temple included Benjamin Cohen, Assistant Secretary General, U.N. (center); Dr. D. G. Vinod, University of Poona, India; Rev. John Haynes Holmes, New York Community Church; Judge Ralph C. Roper, executive vice-president; Rev. Richard Evans, Parliament chairman; Abdelmonen Shaker, Moslem teacher, Cairo, Egypt; Roland Gammon, vice-president, Association of Universalist Men; Dr. Henry C. Carpenter, Protestant Council.

generally speaking, number more followers today than ever before. Some religions, like India's Vedanta, heretofore confined to their own people, are now spreading beyond their borders. Vedanta believes that man is divine. As man develops and becomes spiritual, he more and more realizes his oneness with divinity. That, says Vedanta, is the eternal religion, the background of all religions. There is no antagonism between it and the other great religions. With the Emperor Aśoka it says: "The basis of all religions is the same."

The favorite analogy when speaking of the numerical diversity of the great religions is the parable of the six blind men and the elephant. As they came in contact with the huge animal, and felt with their hands different parts of it, they began to dispute violently as to what it was they were examining. One who caught the end of the tail said it was a rope. One who felt the trunk declared it was a great python. The one who felt the ear said it was a large fan, a fourth, who touched the abdomen, announced it was a drum, the fifth, stroking a leg, maintained it was a pillar, and he who touched a tusk was certain it was a pestle. A seventh man, a passer-by who could see, explained the truth: It was a living being and what they touched were but parts or aspects of the whole. Millions of people in India repeat these words in a famous hymn:

"As the different streams, having their sources in different places, all mingle their water in the sea, so, O Lord, the different paths which men take through different tendencies, various though they appear, crooked or straight, all lead to Thee."

In sum, Truth is one; sages call it by various names.

# PICTURE CREDITS

Page 8: Almasy, Three Lions; 10-11: Dungan, Pix; 12: Vandivert, *Life;* 13: Wide World; 14-15: Dungan, Pix; 16: Cartier-Bresson, Magnum; 17: Keystone and Planet News; 18: Eliot Elisofon, *Life;* 20: Keystone; 21: Almasy, Three Lions; Dungan and Blau, Pix; 22-23: Cartier-Bresson, Magnum; 24: Dungan, Pix; 25: Cartier-Bresson and Acme; 26-28: Dungan; 29: Almasy, Three Lions; 30: Cartier-Bresson; 31: Dungan; 32: Maraini, Monkmeyer; 34: East-West from Black Star and Wide World; 35-37: Cartier-Bresson; 38-39: East-West from Black Star; 40: Ewing Galloway; 42: Cartier-Bresson; 43: Pix and Cartier-Bresson; 44-45: Graphic House; 46: Dungan, Pix and Pan American; 47: Ewing Galloway and Costa, Black Star; 48: Dmitri Kessel, *Life;* 49: Wide World and Costa, Black Star; 50: Metro; 51: Graphic House; 52: Kessel, *Life;* 54: Cartier-Bresson, Magnum; 56: Kessel, *Life;* 57: INP; 58: Tager, Black Star and Gutmann, Pix; 59-60: Cartier-Bresson; 61: Ewing Galloway; 62: China Film, Paul Guillumette and Hildenbrand, Black Star; 63: Ewing Galloway; 64: Ewing Galloway and Blau, Pix; 65: Blau, Pix; 66-67: Cartier-Bresson; 68: CNS-Paul Guillumette; 69: Cartier-Bresson; 70: Alexanderson, Guillumette and Henle, Monkmeyer; 71: Cartier-Bresson and CNS-Paul Guillumette; 72: White Bros., Monkmeyer; 74: Helen Fischer; 76: Gutmann, Pix and Cartier-Bresson; 77: Gutmann, Pix; 78-79: Cartier-Bresson; 80-81: Ewing Galloway; 82: European and Ewing Galloway; 83: Cartier-Bresson; 84: Pan American; 85: Ewing Galloway; 86: Henle, Monkmeyer and Graphic House; 87: Graphic House; 88: Cartier-Bresson; 90: Burton Holmes, Ewing Galloway; 91: Three Lions; 92: Bischof, Magnum; 94: Philip Gendreau and Three Lions; 95: Bischof, Magnum; 96: Dominis, East-West and Camera Clix; 97: Three Lions; 98: Fred Braitsch, FPG, Ewing Galloway; 99: Horace Bristol, Black Star; 100: Underwood & Underwood, Tiers, Monkmeyer; 101: Gendreau; 102: Bischof, Magnum; 103: Three Lions and Horace Bristol; 104: Three Lions and Ewing Galloway; 105: Tiers, Monkmeyer and Horace Bristol; 106: Philip Gendreau; 108: Cartier-Bresson; 109: Weber, Monkmeyer; 110: Satyan, Black Star; 111: Metro and Satyan, Black Star; 112-115: Cartier-Bresson; 116: Gendreau and Cartier-Bresson, Magnum; 117: Cartier-Bresson; 118: Jim Burke, *Life;* 119: Cartier-Bresson; 120: Cartier-Bresson and Dickason, Ewing Galloway; 121: British Information Services; 122: Culver; 123-125: Camera Clix; 126-127: Richter, European; 128: Dickason, Ewing Galloway and Vyarawalla, Pix; 129: European; 130-131: FPG; 132: National Geographic Society and Underwood & Underwood; 133: Ewing Galloway; 134: Cartier-Bresson; 136: Knopf, Pix; 138: Bob Capa, Magnum; 139: *N.Y. Times;* 140-141: Holon, Pix; 142: Capa, Magnum; 143: Camera Clix; 144: Ewing Galloway; 145: Burton Holmes, Ewing Galloway; 146: G. A. Douglas, Gendreau; 147: *Post Dispatch* from Black Star and Philip Gendreau; 148: *Look* Magazine and H. S. Sonnenfeld; 149: W. Braun, P.I.P. and Acme; 150: Sonnenfeld and Weissenstein, Pix; 151: Lisa Larsen, *Life;* 152: George Pickow, Three Lions and Sovfoto; 153: Goldman, Pix and Sonnenfeld; 154: Leni Sonnenfeld and Caps, Pix; 155: David Seymour, Magnum and Keystone; 156: Ewing Galloway; 157: Metro; 158: David D. Duncan, *Life;* 160: William Woodburn; 161: Philip Gendreau; 162: Rapho-Guillumette; 164: George Rodger, Magnum; 165: Graeble, Black Star and Rodger; 166: Marie Mattson; 167: Religious News Service; 168: Izis, Paris-Match and National Council of Churches; 169: Religious News; 170: Pietzsch, Black Star; 171: Jack Birns, *Life;* 172: Evans, Three Lions; 173: Bischof, Magnum; 174: *Look* and Joe Clark, Black Star; 175: *Look;* 176: Bernard Hoffman, *Life* and *Look;* 177: *Look* and Joe Covello, Black Star; 178: Hatch, Pix and *Look;* 179: Cartier-Bresson; 180: Ben & Sid Ross; 181: *Look;* 182: Bob Jones University and Ben Kolvin; 183: Wide World; 184: *Look* and Religious News; 185: Frink, Monkmeyer and John Rose; 186: Jean Speiser and Lucien Aigner, Monkmeyer; 187: *Look;* 188: Roland Gammon; 189: Kosti Ruohomaa, Black Star; 190: Ewing Galloway; 191: Ed Wade, *Parade;* 192: American Airlines, Gendreau, Bob Vose, Black Star; 193: Sargent, A. Devaney and Hoffman, *Life;* 194: Carroll Seghers, Black Star and Religious News; 195: Religious News; 196: Evans, Three Lions; 198: Belin, Rapho-Guillumette; 199: Black Star; 200: Cartier-Bresson; 201: Intercontinentale; 202: Omnia, Three Lions and Brunner, Pix; 203: Pasi, Three Lions and Keystone; 204: Cartier-Bresson; 206: Jean Lyons, Black Star; 207: Black Star; 208: Rapho-Guillumette and Cartier-Bresson; 209: Ernest Rathenau, Pix and Cartier-Bresson; 210: TWA; 211: Gendreau; 212: INP; 213: Enell, Frederick Lewis and Dudognon, Rapho-Guillumette; 214: Cartier-Bresson; 215: Kayfetz, Monkmeyer; 216: Three Lions; 217: Youssef, *Life;* 218: Richard Thomas and Baha'i; 220: Robert Laubach, World Literary and D. Stock, Magnum; 221: Von Matt, Rapho-Guillumette and Wide World; 222: U.N.; 223: George Barris.